DATA ANALYTICS

A Comprehensive Beginner's Guide to Learn the Realms of Data Analytics

Liam Damien

Table of Contents

Introduction

Big data, data science, and data analytics are revolutionizing businesses across the world. Data analytics not only plays an important role in business but also plays an important role in a person's life. For instance, one can use data analytics to make lifestyle choices or to derive some information from a business point of view to increase profits. Since businesses now collect real-time data, it is becoming difficult for them to understand and analyze that data. This is where data analytics comes into the picture.

The information in the book has been organized in a format that will make it easy for you to learn. You can use this book as a reference or a guide to help you improve your understanding of data analytics. Over the course of the book, you will gather information on what data is, and how this data can be analyzed to obtain some information about the future. You will also learn more about how you can use data to improve your business. This book also sheds some light on the different tools and algorithms that you can use for the same. You will learn what data science, big data, and data analytics are, and gather information on different areas of data analytics.

Thank you for purchasing the book. I hope you gather all the information you are looking for.

Chapter 1

What Is Data?

According to the dictionary, data is a collection of facts that include words, numbers, observations, measurements, etc. These facts are fed to the computer in a form that it can process. Regardless of which industry you work in or what your interests are, you may have read numerous articles or content about how data has begun to change the world. These articles could have been about boosting the revenue of a company, helping to cure a disease, or the construction of a more responsible and efficient building or targeting the right advertisements to the right customers.

In simple words, data is information. You should also know that the data that you read about in the news is about Big Data alone, and this data refers to that information which can be read by a machine and not by human beings.

Machine versus Humans

Unstructured data or data that can be read by humans refer to the information that a human being can study or interpret, such as understanding the meaning of a block of text or an image. If a human being can interpret the information that is given to them, then that information or data is human-readable.

Structured data or machine-readable information refers to that information that can be read and processed by computers. Computers process this information through programs, and programs are a set of instructions that are written by a developer. These instructions make it easier for the computer to manipulate the data. When the data is then applied to the right set of programs, you can develop software.

Is The Position Of A Data Scientist The Best Job In The 21st Century?

Once the data is collected, it will need to be cleaned, processed, interpreted, and analyzed in the right way before it can be used to obtain any insights. Regardless of the type of data that you want to use or are talking about, the person who can perform all the functions mentioned above is a data scientist. The position of a data scientist is one of the most sought after positions in this century. An executive who formerly worked at Google believes that the job of a data scientist is the sexiest job in this century.

If you want to become a data scientist, you will need to have a solid foundation in modeling, statistics, computer science, math, and analytics. The role of a data scientist is different from traditional jobs because they have a better understanding of the different business processes. They also know how to communicate the findings to the IT leaders and the business management in a way that will allow them to influence how the organization approaches any business problem or challenge.

Data Resources

If you want to learn more about data collection, big data, and want to learn more about how you can use different books, blogs, events, companies, and more. This book will also shed some light on data analytics and how you can analyze different types of data.

Data Blogs

- The blog Flowing Data has numerous visualizations, tutorials, and resources that can be used to learn more about data analytics. This blog is run by Dr. Nathan Yau. This blog also provides some information on different humorous discussions and the different books that you can read to learn more about data analytics.
- The blog FiveThirtyEight is run by Nate Silver, who is a data wizard. This blog sheds some light on what data analysis is and also provides some information on the different news topics in culture, economics, sports, and politics.
- Edwin Chen is a data scientist working at Dropbox, and he runs a blog that sheds some light on the different algorithms that can be used for analysis.
- Data Science Weekly is a blog that is more like a newspaper and has all the latest news and developments in data science.
- SmartDataCollective is an online data community that is taken care of by Social Media Today. This blog provides

information about the latest trends in data collection, business intelligence, and data management.

- KDnuggets is an online resource that can be used by anyone who has even the slightest interest in data science.
- Data Elixir is a great blog that has all the information to learn more about data. You can sign up to receive a weekly digest that will be sent to your inbox.

Data Influencers

There are numerous people whose social media pages and websites can shed some light on data analytics, and also learn about the new developments in the field of data.

- The CTO of Spark, Marcus Borba, has a feed that is stacked with different complex concepts. He makes it easier for people to understand concepts like NoSQL and the Internet of Things (IoT) by using visualization.
- Lillian Pierson, the author of the book Data Science for Dummies, has a lot of information and articles about Big Data. She has numerous articles, news clips, blog posts, and other information that will provide readers with information on business space and data science.
- Kirk Borne, who is the Principal Data Scientist at the company BoozAllen, often posts links and retweets those links to some articles on Data Science and Big Data.

Chapter 2

Where Can I Find the Required Data?

In this day and age, information and data play an important role. Data is being collected and accumulated at an overwhelming pace. This data could be stored in databases or data warehouses or could be scattering across as unstructured data in the form of documents, emails, audiovisual files, and text messages.

It is important to know what data type you have collected – whether the data is structured or unstructured, static or dynamic, behavioral or attitudinal – in order to have a better position to understand the data and analyze it. When you learn to categorize your data, you will be able to understand what processes you can use to make sure that your predictive analytics efforts work.

The easiest way to define the efforts is in terms of the tools you will be using. Predictive analytics uses tools, techniques, and algorithms to analyze business data. It uses algorithms of three disciplines – statistics, data mining, and machine learning. These tools and techniques are used to build predictive models. Different chapters in the book cover these disciplines extensively. When a predictive model is built carefully, it can help the user understand and spot patterns and trends that represent the best business opportunities. It is always better to understand the relationship between predictive analytics and the three disciplines in order to strengthen your analysis.

There are two ways to implement predictive analytics:

- Data-Driven: As the name suggests, this approach is solely based on your data.
- User-Driven: This approach explores the different ideas you may have about your customers and their behavior and also examines whether your data supports the ideas that you have.

Recognizing the Data Types

If your company or business is just like every other company or business, you can easily gather a vast amount of historical data. Most of this data could be found in data warehouses or databases, while some may be scattered across the hard drives of the computers used in the business. Your raw data can, therefore, consist of emails, text files, presentations, audio and video files, images, and emails.

This sheer amount of data could be overwhelming. It is only when you categorize the data that you create the core of your predictive analytics model. The more you learn about the data, the better you will be able to use it and analyze it to benefit your company. You can initially work with improving your knowledge on different data types before you work with identifying the core of your model.

Structured and Unstructured Data

Data that is contained in documents, databases, data warehouses, emails, and other data files can be categorized either as unstructured or structured data.

Structured data is data that are organized. The data always follow a consistent order and are always easy to search. This data can be accessed easily and understood by any person or machine.

A classic example would be the data that is found in an Excel sheet. Each data set has labeled columns. This data is always consistent. The column headers that are a brief description of the data found in it tell you exactly what kind of content can be found in each column. In a column that is labeled images, you can no doubt find images in the column. This consistency always ensures that structured data is amenable to automated data management.

Structured data is often stored in databases and data warehouses in well – defined schemas. The data is often stored in a tabular form with columns and rows that define the exact attributes of the data.

Unstructured data is of free – form. It is often dispersed and never found in a tabular form. This type of data is often not easily retrievable, and such data takes a lot of time to be understood. Numerous emails, web pages, documents, and files all in scattered locations are classic examples of unstructured data.

It is impossible to categorize such data since it is often created in an unstructured manner. This makes it difficult to understand the different attributes of the data, which is why it takes a lot of time to group this data.

The content that is obtained from unstructured data is often hard to work with or even make sense of using programs. Most computer programs find it difficult to analyze or generate reports on such data without being able to process it since the data lacks structure. There are newer technologies being developed which would be able to make sense of the unstructured data.

It is true that there is more unstructured data in the world when compared to structured data. Since it takes more work to make unstructured data usable, it tends to grasp the most attention and also takes more time. It is no wonder that the promise of a machine or a program being able to process and analyze unstructured data is a huge selling point for any predictive analytics model.

You have to remember never to underestimate unstructured data and how powerful it is to your analysis. It is always more efficient to analyze structured data as opposed to analyzing unstructured data since the latter would be costlier to process when you are building a predictive analytics model. The selection of the data, its relevance to your analysis, cleansing, and also the subsequent transformations are often lengthy and tedious tasks. It is only after the data has been through all these processes, which make it worth using a predictive analytics model.

It is often easier to get results using structured data as opposed to using unstructured data since you will never have to worry about there being a delay in the scrubbing process.

Tagging documents and text analytics are two ways to structure unstructured text documents, grouping, summarizing the data, and also linking their content. This will also help the user uncover any hidden patterns in the data. It is also important to notice that most search engine platforms often provide tools to index data and also make it searchable.

Unstructured data does not often lack structure; it just takes a little more effort to understand the structure. Every text in any digital file does have some structure that is associated with it, and it often shows up in the metadata. This applies to every other form of structured data.

It may be worthwhile to conduct a thorough analysis of the structural components of the data in order to estimate the potential value of any analysis that is conducted on the unstructured data. When the analysis provides a little insight into the data, you should try to determine the resources you will need to allocate to analyze that portion of unstructured data.

The idea is that you can always find some order in the data you have collected. You will definitely need to do a lot of digging into the data to understand it better. The content in a bunch of emails between two people may definitely stray away from the original subject of the emails, although the subject line stays the same. There are times when the subject line may not even make sense.

The line that separates the two types of data is not always clear since there are some aspects of unstructured data that are similar to those of structured data. Whether or not that structure reflects the content of the data is unclear on most occasions. For that matter, structured data can also hold some unstructured data within it. For instance, in a web form, users may have to give feedback by choosing answers from multiple-choice questions and also provided with a comment box where they can provide feedback in text form. This comment field is unstructured data because the information is in free – form. These cases are often considered a mixture of both structured and unstructured data.

There will always be some exceptions in the field of defining data since the definitions of the two types of data could be blurry. There is always a way to make the distinction between the data.

Static and Dynamic Data

Data can also be identified as static, dynamic, or a mix of the two. Dynamic or streamed data change continuously. For instance, the constant updates on Twitter, Facebook, and the changes in the stock market while the market is still open. This data changes continuously.

Static data, on the other hand, is self – contained and is enclosed. The problems that are associated with this type of data include outliers, gaps, incorrect data, or all of these because of which this type of data would need to be cleansed and prepared before it is used for analysis.

With streamed data, other kinds of problems may arise. The sheer volume of streamed data could be overwhelming since there is a constant inflow of data. If the data is streamed in faster, then there would be a difficulty in analyzing the data accurately.

There are two models that are often used to analyze streamed data:

Examine the newest data points only and then make a decision about the next dataset that will come in using the model. This is an incremental approach since it helps to build a picture of the data as it arrives.

Evaluate the entire dataset and then make a decision each time a new data point comes in. This approach is inclusive of different data points in the analysis and helps the user understand what data points caused a change in the result.

You can choose one of these models over the other depending on the nature of your business and how an anticipated impact would affect your business decision.

There are a few business domains, which value the arrival of real-time data. All this data will need to be analyzed since it is being streamed. You must also check and verify that the data is interpreted immediately and accurately. The model will redraw the entire representation of the world using the information that is newly available. In doing so, you can obtain results that are up – to – date.

For instance, a predictive analytics model will be able to process the stock prices as a data feed and also analyze the data even when it constantly changes. The model will be able to analyze the conditions of the market an also help one decide what stocks to trade-in.

It is clear that the process of analyzing streamed data differs from static data. It gets difficult to analyze data that is of both types. Often the learning and building of any model are based on static data. It is only when that model is deployed to being used will it begin to process streamed data. Static data is also often refreshed through regular updates.

Identifying Different Data Categories

When companies have been in the industry for some time, they will have gathered a vast amount of information and data about their customers and their business. This process is called business intelligence. In order to help you develop and identify categories for your data, there are a few categories of data that have been provided below, which will help you do the same.

Behavioral data is often derived from transactions that take place on a regular basis in the business. These data can be collected automatically:

- Items bought

- Items purchased on sale
- Modes of payment
- Customers' information:
- Name
- Phone Number
- Email Address
- Address

We have all provided such information when we make purchases online. Other types of data that can be collected from customers with their cooperation is:

- Data filled out on surveys
- Answers to polls and questionnaires
- Information collected when customers directly make a purchase from the company
- Over the phone
- Physical Store
- Through the company's website

In addition to this, there are different types of data that can be collected by businesses from their operations, which can provide a lot of information about their customers. The common examples for these include the time a customer spends on a website and also their browsing history. All the data that is collected can be used to answer a variety of questions:

- How can the business improve a customer's experience?

- How can the business retain existing customers and also attract new ones?
- What would your customers like to buy next?
- What products can you recommend to any of your customers?

The first step towards answering these questions would be to collect data from the customer-related operations and analyze that data comprehensively. The data types that combine to create such data often intersect and can be described or grouped differently in order to analyze that data.

Most companies collect different types of data by giving every customer personalized experience. For instance, a business can provide customers with tools that can be used to build personalized websites that would empower the customers and also enrich their experience. It also allows businesses to learn more about their customer's wants and needs through this approach.

The ability to combine different types of data from a number of sources is why predictive analytics can yield useful results and insights.

Attitudinal Data

Any information that can help the business understand how customers could think or feel is considered attitudinal data.

When companies issue surveys asking their customers for feedback and their thoughts about the different products provided by the business, the collected data would be categorized as attitudinal data.

This data has a direct impact on the marketing campaign that the company can launch in order to attract more customers. It also helps the business shape the aim and the message of the company. This type of data can also help make the message and the products more relevant to the customers' needs and desires. This will help the business serve the existing customers better and also attract new ones.

The limitation of this data is its imperfection since not every customer would answer questions objectively. Most customers also do not provide relevant details that may have shaped their decisions on why they purchased that particular product.

Most customers use social media platforms to express their satisfaction or dissatisfaction about a product, company, or service. The opinions of those customers reflect their interaction with the company and their experiences. As a result, most companies that are gathering data apply different types of analysis to understand it. One of the most sought-after analysis is sentiment analysis or opinion mining. Facebook posts, tweets, or other updates are often analyzed to understand the attitude of the customer. The results obtained from this analysis help the business decisions in what way they can improve their services.

Most businesses may find it challenging to identify and collect attitudinal data, and it can also be difficult to match transactional data with social media data. It is often a very difficult task to link various data sources in a meaningful way.

Behavioral Data

This type of data helps the company identify what customers do when they interact with the business. The data often consists only of data from various transactions that take place between the business and the customer. The data is more reliable when compared to attitudinal data since it represents what actually took place. Businesses will know what products they are selling, the customers who are buying them, and also identifying how customers pay for them.

This type of data is a by-product of operations that take place normally and is available to the company at no extra cost. Attitudinal data always requires surveys to be conducted or even conduct market research to understand the customers better.

Attitudinal data is always analyzed to understand why customers behave the way they do and also understand how they feel about the business. Behavioral data, on the other hand, tells you what is happening and also helps you understand the customers' real-time actions. The former provides an insight into the motivations of the customers while behavioral data provides the 'who – did – what' aspect of the business. Your analysis will need to include both types of data since they are complementary.

Combining both types of data will make predictive analytics models more accurate since the business will be able to define the segments of the customer base, offer more personalized customer experiences and also identify the drivers behind the business.

Demographic Data

Demographic data comprises information that includes race, age, education level, marital status, household income, employment status, and also location. You can always obtain this information from the Census Bureau and other government agencies. You can also obtain this information through certain commercial entities.

The more information you have about your customers, the better insight you will have to identify certain demographic and market trends as well as trying to understand how these trends could affect your business. It is important for a business to measure the pulse of these trends in order to adjust to the changes and also to attract newer customers.

The customers can be divided into different segments, and each segment is interested in different products. Small businesses that cater to specific locations should always pay attention to any changes that may occur in that location. Populations have always been changing over time in a number of neighborhoods. It is important for businesses to be aware of such things since these changes will affect the business significantly.

Demographic data, when combined with attitudinal and behavioral data, allows businesses to paint an accurate picture of their customers and also of their potential customers. This will allow businesses to increase satisfaction, acquisition, and retention. This data is static, making it hard to predict the change in behavior when the underlying variables do not change. Therefore, this data is only useful when it is combined with transactional data.

Generating Predictive Analytics

There are two models one can use to generate and implement predictive analytics, based purely on your data with absolutely no prior knowledge of what conclusions you are after. You could also do the same with a proposed business hypothesis, which the data may or may not support. You do not have to make a decision on the type of model you would want to choose – these approaches can be used together too. Each approach has its advantages and disadvantages.

Whether you are using hypotheses to test and analyze the data that comes out of your analysis or examining your data with no prior assumptions set of what you may find, the goal is the same: always to decide whether or not to act on what you find. You have an active role in implementing the processes that are needed for either approach to predictive analytics. Both approaches have their limitations. It is important to understand which approach works best for the company.

When you combine both types of analysis, it empowers the business and also enables the business to expand. It also helps the business understand its customers better and will also help the business make better decisions and also increase the profits of the company.

Data-Driven Analytics

If you base your analysis purely on the data you have collected, you can always use internal data, which could have been accumulated by the business over the years. It could also be external data that could be relevant to your business. This type of data is often purchased from a third party.

In order to make sense of that data, the business can use data mining tools in order to overcome the overwhelming size of the data. These models could also be used to reveal certain patterns you may not have been aware of. The model can also help the business uncover some relationships within the data. Businesses can use this information to generate new categories of data and could also gather new understanding and insights. Data-driven analysis can always reveal certain gems that could be used to improve the business.

Data-driven analytics is a technique that is suited for large volumes of data since it is impossible for human beings to interpret and analyze these volumes of data. Different visualization techniques and data mining tools make it easier for businesses to understand the data better since the models help users cut their data into smaller fragments. The following general principles will need to be kept in mind:

- The outcome of the analysis is dependent on the complexity of the data set. If the data contains some vital information about the variables that the business is trying to study, and the business collects the required information for a long period, the business can learn from the data.

- This type of analysis is neutral since:
    - o There is no need for any prior knowledge
    - o The business is not basing its analysis on any specific hypotheses, and the analysis is being conducted with just the general goal in mind.
    - o There is no bias or a specific objective behind the analysis, which allows users to look at numerous aspects. This method is termed as random and broad data mining.
    - o If you conduct such an analysis, and you also identify something new about the business. It will also become easier to determine if the results obtained from the analysis can be implemented.

Relying only on data-driven analytics adds a lot of risk to the business decisions that will be made. The risk can, however, be limited or mitigated by incorporating some characteristics of user-driven analytics. When the real-world data proves that the data you have used is accurate, the decision made is appropriate.

The following story is extremely interesting. It talks about how data can help the business decide instead of letting the business be the sole driver in the decision-making process. Amazon and Netflix look at vast amounts of data in their guests to create the best shows in the industry. Based on the insights obtained from the data, Amazon created a show called "Alpha House," which did alright in comparison to Netflix's "House of Cards," which gained immense popularity. What do you think created an impact on the outcome of the shows? It turns out that Netflix used the results obtained from data analysis to understand their customers' needs better, after which a team of experts created a show that catered to the interests of the customers. Amazon, on the other hand, relied only on the data and data analysis and produced a show that their audience would like. The result was that the show that Amazon produced was successful but not a blockbuster.

Data can only help a little when it comes to making the decision-making process a success. The management will need to make the best decision based on what they would have learned from the data.

User-Driven Analysis

In a user-driven analysis, the managers of the business conceive ideas and try to test those ideas by using the right data. The test data does not always have to be vast – it could be something that could be defined by the business and also chosen by the business to test their ideas.

It is important that certain guidelines and meticulous planning are done to ensure that the right data sets and the correct methods have been chosen to perform the analysis. It is important to select the variables that have the power to predict. This can be a daunting and time-consuming process. It is, therefore, important that the business understands that the predictive analytics concept is crucial.

It is important for one to learn more about the business or the problem in hand, and also develop strategic thinking abilities to back up the hypothesis. Intuition and vision can be most helpful here. You will need to remember that the business is looking for information on how the data will support the ideas that the management has. This approach limits the definition of predictive analytics to the ideas that are being probed. It is easier to make decisions when you have the right data to back you up.

When you rely on user-driven analytics, there is a possibility that you may miss the hidden relationships that lie within the data. Your ideas may often miss the subtle changes that occur in the data collected over time. These changes often come to light only when the business used data-driven analytics.

In short, your ideas should always include a term that would describe the unknowns that surround your business and also probe those unknowns to look for any interconnected variables in different aspects of the business. This is often hard to achieve, but data-driven analysis can help here. For instance, you may analyze the importance of the amount you spend on the raw material you will need to create your product, the demand for that product, and also how the costs you incur during production will affect the price of your product. There is a possibility that you may miss out on certain hidden factors that could be correlated to one another or may have an influence on the pricing of your product, such as the economy, the turnover of the employees, and the business and on how the product is being consumed.

The process of probing the ideas the management of a business has may not be as straightforward as analyzing an entire dataset. This process could also be affected by the management's bias to prove the accuracy of their assumptions.

Once the data is obtained and categorized as necessary, it is essential that the business identify the right models to work with the data. Predictive analytics models can be created with either a preset goal in mind or with a goal that is dynamic. The models that are built with a preset goal are often easy to build and easy to fix if there are any bugs. It is the model with dynamic goals in it that is difficult to understand and build. The latter models are often more useful since the aims of the business may change with respect to a change in the customers' likes and dislikes.

Chapter 3

The Types of Analytics

We have discussed what analytics is, and information has been provided on the different challenges and risks that are faced in the analytics industry. This chapter will give you a brief introduction to the different types of analytics. In this way, you will be able to get a good idea of the type of analytics you can use in your business.

You should now understand that the idea behind data analytics is to obtain insight and to help you make better decisions when it comes to business. That said, the methods that you use to create business technologies or even design data analytics processes would vary.

It is extremely critical when it comes to building designs to build a data warehouse or even the architecture for a business intelligence process. You will also need to provide a multifaceted system. You will be able to optimize the processing of data and will also be able to analyze diverse and large data sets. There are four types of analytics. We will discuss each type for a better understanding.

Predictive Analytics

This type of analytics is always used for forecasting. Here, the data is always turned into information that is valuable and can be easily used. You will be able to use this data to determine the future or even the outcome of a certain event in the future. You will also be able to estimate the likelihood of an event occurring.

This type of analytics comprises numerous statistical techniques that are often used for modeling, data mining, computer learning, and game theory. You will be able to use these techniques to analyze the data that has been obtained in the present and also use the historical data to make certain predictions about events in the future.

When you are looking at predictive analytics from the perspective of business, you will find that the models always help you capture the relationship between numerous factors and parameters that affect the data. You will be able to assess the risk that is associated with the factors and parameters. You can assess the conditions properly and will also be able to make guided decisions.

There are three basic processes that are included in predictive analytics, which are:

1. Predictive Modeling

2. Decision Analysis and Optimization

3. Transaction Profiling

Let me give you a couple of examples of how you can use predictive analytics in business. Let us assume that your business focuses solely on optimizing and managing the relationship you have with customers. You will be able to analyze all the data you have on the customers and will also be able to expose any patterns that exist in the behavior of customers.

Let us look at another example. Let us assume that your company offers customers multiple products. You will be able to identify the amount that the consumers were willing to spend on your products and will also be able to understand the usage of the products or any other behavior. This will help you make efficient sales that will create effective returns. This will lead to greater profitability because you will be able to build stronger relationships with your customers.

Every organization will need to invest a certain amount of money in a team of experts who will be able to create statistical algorithms to find and analyze the data that is relevant to the question in mind. The data analytics team always works with the leaders in the business industry to construct a design to analyze data using predictive information.

Descriptive Analytics
This is a process that is used in data mining and business intelligence. In descriptive analytics, you will be able to look at data and also analyze past events. You will be able to obtain insight into approaching the events that may occur in the future. You will use

this process to analyze and mine through the data to determine the reasons why the business has either succeeded or failed in the past. Every department in the company would always use this type of analysis to understand their successes and failures.

Through descriptive models, you will be able to analyze the different relationships in the data and also quantify the same. This type of analytics is always used to classify and group consumers. The descriptive models are very different from predictive models. They try to identify the relationship that exists between the products and services your company offers and the consumers. Descriptive models do not rank the customers based on one particular action.

You will be able to use the descriptive models to categorize the customers you have based on the products that they prefer and also their loyalty towards your company. You will also be able to develop further models that will help you process big data and make predictions for the future.

For instance, you could try to analyze the usage of electricity over the years in the area you live in, which will help you plan your power usage in order to have a lower cost.

Prescriptive Analytics
Prescriptive analytics works towards optimizing and simulating the data and creating a model for the future. This type of analytics helps in synthesizing big data and will also help you understand the rules of business to help you make predictions about the future.

This process is something that has gone beyond just predicting the outcomes of the future. You will be able to suggest the action that would help your company benefit from the predictions that you have made from the data. You will better understand the implications of every decision you make while also understanding what event will occur when it will occur, and why it will occur.

You will understand the different decision options and also take advantage of a certain event that may transpire in the future while working towards mitigating the risk. You will also understand the implication of the decisions you will be making. You will be able to process new data and improve your futuristic predictions to help you make better decisions.

This type of analytics will work towards combining business rules, mathematical models, and data. The data could always be inputted through multiple sources, both external and internal. You could obtain different types of data, such as categorical, nominal, ordinal, numerical, and unstructured data. You will need to use the business processes to understand the preferences, policies, boundaries, and the best practices in the decisions you make for your business. You will be able to develop mathematical models using the mathematical sciences that also include applied statistics.

For instance, when using prescriptive analytics, you could benefit the healthcare industry by helping the industry plan strategically. You can use the data you have obtained using external factors. Such data includes population, demographic trends, population health

trends, and economic data. You would be able to plan for future investments in capital and know whether or not you will be able to expand your business.

The other examples that you could consider are the utility and energy industries. Gas has been priced based on the demography. You will find the prices fluctuating based on econometrics, supply, demand, weather, and geopolitics. You will be able to use this type of analytics t0 predict the prices of gas using internal and external variables. This would enable you to gather a list of decision options that will help you make the right decision.

Diagnostic Analytics

Diagnostics analytics is very different from descriptive analytics in the sense that it focuses on trying to identify why a specific thing has happened and not on what has happened. This type of analytics will always look for the causes or the processes that led to the results. Let us look at an example of diagnostics analytics – the revenue in the East Coast has increased, and the reason behind this is that there is an increase in the employment of professionals, closure of major competition in the area, and the investment and change in the marketing approach. It is important to remember that descriptive analytics cannot be used to obtain the answer to some important questions like "How can this solution be replicated?" or "What methods can be followed to overcome this problem?" The answer to these questions is provided through diagnostic analytics.

Diagnostic analytics is used widely in sports. For example, there are numerous teams that have stopped assessing their pitchers in the team based on the number of runs that they give the other team. Based on that data, we can say that there is a direct relationship between the number of runs that the pitchers allow and the rate of their strikeouts. It is for this reason that baseball teams are now looking at understanding the process so that they can assess the players in their team better.

Chapter 4

Introduction to Big Data

Data that is obtained from two significantly different sources are grouped under the banner of Big Data. The first source of data is the data that is found within the organization or business, and that is shared across a vast network. This data includes PDF documents, blogs, emails, work documents, business events, internal files, process events, and any other structured data, unstructured or semi-structured data that can be found within the organization. The second source of data would be the data that is available outside the organization. Most of this information is available for free, but there is some information that would require a certain payment to be made in order to obtain it. Most of this information is available to the general public, but there is some information that is considered confidential and is kept within the organization itself. This information includes literature on products that are distributed by the competitors, information available on social media, hints from third parties, certain organization hierarchies, and also any complaints that may have been posted by customers on regulatory sites.

You may begin to wonder what makes Big Data any different from the data that is being used since ancient times. There are four characteristics of Big Data that make is very different from other kinds of data – Volume, Velocity, Variety, and Veracity. There are a number of other characteristics that differentiate Big Data from other types of data, but these are the most important and prominent characteristics to consider.

Volume

Numerous organizations have started to struggle with the amount of data that is being stored in their data warehouses since big data took the world by a storm. It was noted in the Fortune magazine that the world had already created close to 10 exabytes of data by the year 2006 and that this number would double by the year 2015. It has also been identified that this amount of data can now be collected within a few nanoseconds, thereby increasing the data collected by trillion gigabytes every hour that is a scary amount of data.

A few years ago, there were organizations that would count their data storage space for any analytics in terabytes. Now, they can only do the same in petabytes since the data collected has doubled or tripled since then. The amount of data does cause a strain on the analytics architecture for different organizations in different industries. For instance, let us consider an organization that is in the communication industry. You know that this organization would definitely have a hundred million customers. If data were collected for these customers on a daily basis, there would be at least five petabytes of data in a hundred days. Most companies try to get rid of data daily, but regulators have asked most companies in the communication industry to store records about calls made or the data used by each customer.

Velocity

Velocity can be understood from two different perspectives – one that represents latency while the other represents the throughput of data. Let us first take a look at latency. The analytics infrastructure was once a store – and – report environment where the data that was collected the previous day was used to make reports, and this data was represented as "D-1". Over the last decade, the analytics infrastructure has been used in different business processes that there was a necessity to change the infrastructure to cater to the needs of all businesses. For example, some advertising agencies are trying to conduct analytics to help them place advertisements on online platforms within ten milliseconds.

Let us now consider the second measure of velocity – the throughput of data. This represents the data that is flowing through the pipes of the analytics infrastructure. The amount of global mobile data is growing at the rate of 80 percent, which is said to compound annually, implying that the data that is collected annually is set to increase by 12 – 14 exabytes per year as users begin to share more images and videos with the world. In order to analyze this data, many corporates are seeking analytical infrastructure that will help them process information in parallel.

Variety

It was in the late 1990s that Data Warehouse Technology was introduced to create and represent data using Meta–models that would help to simplify data and also help to represent data collected in one form, irrespective of whether or not the data was structured.

The data was often compiled from multiple sources and was then transformed using either ETL (Extract, Transform, Load) or ELT (Extract data, load it into the warehouse and transform the data within the warehouse). The idea was to narrow down the variety and ambiguity in the data collected and also structure that data to put it to good use. Big Data has helped to expand our horizons by enabling new data integration and solutions infrastructure and data analytics technology. A number of call center analytics constantly seek solutions that would help them attend to their customers better. These solutions would also help them understand the conversation that takes place between them and the disgruntled customer, which would then give them an idea of how to proceed further. The source data that is obtained from call centers are only unstructured data like audio, sound, or text, and some structured data. Different applications gather different types of data from blogs, emails, and documents. For example, Slice, a company used to provide analytics for online orders, uses raw data that comes from a number of different organizations like online bookstore purchases, airline tickets, parking tickets, music download receipts, and any other purchases that may have hit your email. How can this information be normalized into creating product catalogs and also analyze any purchases made?

Veracity

Internal data is often carefully governed, while Big Data comes from a number of sources that are outside the control of the company, and this data often comes with a lot of inaccuracies and incorrectness, which would hamper the analysis made. Veracity represents the sustainability of the data obtained and also looks for the credibility of the sources of data that are obtained for a target audience.

Let us try to see how we can understand the credibility of the sources of data. If organizations began to collect information on their own products using third parties and then provide that information to their customer care support or their contact center employees in order to support the queries that customers have, the organizations providing the information would need to be assessed and screened before trusting the information that is provided by them. Otherwise, there can be a possibility of the organization making a wrong offer to the customer, thereby affecting the revenue. Numerous social media responses to different campaigns could come from unhappy customers or disgruntled employees, which would definitely impact the decisions made by the company. For instance, if there was a survey conducted by companies on the products provided by them and customers happened to like the product, this would be taken into consideration. If the customer were to select an option that did not show that they liked the product, it is important to know why before taking this unstructured piece of data into account.

We always have to consider the amount of truth that can be shared with an audience. The veracity of the data that is collected or created within a given organization is often considered to be well-intentioned. Some of that data cannot be shared with the public since there could be some threat to the company. This would reduce the chance of having a wider communication network. For instance, if customer service has provided the manufacturing and engineering department with the shortcomings of a particular product based on the feedback given by customers, the data shared should be selective and, on a need, – to – know basis only. Other data can be shared with some customers who have certain prerequisites or contracts.

Big Data makes it possible for numerous businesses to process all the information that is collected on the simple learning systems. They would need to identify one signal from all the noise. It is only through this way of learning that it is possible to translate sentences from one language to the other. Parallelism and processing enable systems to take up thousands of pieces of evidence and then test them independently before adding up the results.

Drivers for Big Data
The creation of Big Data has been rapidly increasing over the years. This section looks at the forces that drove the rapid creation of Big Data. Three factors majorly contribute to the establishment of Big Data – automation, monetization, and consumers. It is this interaction between these three forces that have increased the speed of creating Big Data.

When the automation of data increases, it is easier to offer Big Data creation and also improve the consumption opportunities of consumers, while the monetization process helps to provide an efficient market for Big Data.

Sophisticated Customers

The increase in the level of information available and the associated tools to work with that information has created a new set of sophisticated clients. These consumers are all experts at using technology and statistics, far more analytic and more connected to the world through social media than the customers from a decade ago. These clients know where to source the data from and what one can do with that data.

The world we live in is full of marketing messages, and while most marketing still happens in magazines, newspapers, radio, network TV, and even in conventional media, the narrowcasting of advertisements is gaining more popularity. This can be seen in the local ads in magazines, the insertion of commercials on set-top boxes, and the use of information from commuters to change the street display advertisements. The world of the Internet has become personalized. Electronic yellow pages, search engines, and social network sites all have ads that are unique to a particular segment of the public or an individual. Cookies on the Internet are all being used to track the behavior of the users and also create content based on the said behavior.

Text messages and emails have rapidly led to interpersonal interactions. Communication has not started with only marketers but has also started between friends and third parties and has expanded to group chats, bulletin boards, and social media which would allow people to converse about their intentions and what they would like to purchase, their expectations, fears, and their disappointments with small and large groups. Unlike text messages and emails, a conversation that happens on the Internet is available for most people to read either now or later.

So far, we have only been looking at communication in a single form. Other sources combine all the information that is available in more than one media. For instance, Facebook conversations often involve some media, including sound clips, text, video, and photos. Alternative reality and second world information are both becoming exciting areas to try out product ideas in a world where product usage can be worked on and experimented with.

Most often, we need experts who would help us understand and sort out product features and how those features would relate to our usage of those products. Some experts are available to help us understand our usage, pricing, and quality and also provide us with valuable information on the products. Numerous marketers are encouraging ambassadors or advisor programs using social media as their platform. These selected customers will always receive a preview of the new products that are being created and also actively participate in evaluating and promoting the product. It is true that the people we know and trust often sway the decisions we make.

This is why social media is the biggest contributor to advertising and marketing. Social media has helped bring consumers together and has helped them share the experiences that assist them in making objective decisions about products.

Consumers form groups on social media and use different modes of communication – messages, emails, Facebook Messenger, Instagram, emails, and so on. It is always interesting to see how the leaders, consumers who lead the entire social group, sway the statistics.

There are numerous ways to utilize these social networks to influence the reuse and purchase of these products.

Studying Consumer Experience
Most of the data collected are often unstructured. The data obtained from analyzing the text for intensity, sentiments, readership, referrals, related blogs, and any other information can be used to organize the data into negative and positive influences and also assess the impact of those influences on the consumer base.

Organizing Customer Experience
Numerous reviews can be provided to prospective consumers, which would help them evaluate the product they want to purchase.

Influencing Social Networks
Marketing material, company directions, product changes, and celebrity endorsements on social media would help control the likes and dislikes of prospective consumers.

Feedback on operations, marketing or products

When organizations use information that is generated via social media, rapid changes can be made to the product mix to help improve how products are marketed to prospective consumers.

Society has played a significant role in the way the production process has been evaluated. The Internet and social networks have altered the access to information. A consumer could choose to "love" a product on Facebook, and every friend on the user's list would have instant access to this information. The same goes for every other social media platform.

Automation

Kiosks, Interactive Voice Response (IVR), email, mobile devices, chats, third- party applications, corporate websites, and social networks have helped generate a fair amount of information about the customers. In addition to this, the interaction that exists between consumers on different media can now be organized and analyzed. The biggest change lies in the organization's ability to modify the experience of customers using procedures, software policies, and personalization, which would make self-service customer friendly.

The sales and marketing departments in most organizations have received the biggest boost in instrumentation since they began to use Internet-driven automation. Shopping, browsing, ordering, and customer service on the Internet not only has provided users with tremendous control but has also created a massive flood of information to the product, marketing, and sales departments of the company to understand the behavior of a potential or existing buyer. Each sequence of clicks on the Internet can be collated, collected, and analyzed to understand a customer's delight, dysphoria, puzzlement, or even outright defection. A lot more information can be obtained using the sequence to understand the decisions that consumers make.

Self-service has started to creep in through different means: kiosks, IVRs, handheld devices, and numerous others. Each of these means of communication acts as a huge pool of time-and-motion studies. There is data that is available on the number of steps customers had taken, the products they have compared, and attributes that they focus on – price, brand, features, defects, comparisons, and so on.

Suppliers and retailers have obtained large amounts of data from the electronic sensors and self-service parts that are connected to the customer reactions to products. If a consumer uses a two-way set-top box at home, the supplier would have the ability to understand the channel surfing behavior of these users. Some questions can be answered through the data collected: Did the consumer change the channel when advertisements started? Did the user turn the volume down when a jingle began to play? When the user uses the Internet to shop for a product, the click stream can be used and analyzed to study his or her shopping behavior. How many products did the consumer look at? Did the user look at the product description or the price when he or she was watching the product? This set of data would help the supplier understand and analyze the consumer to the smallest detail.

What are the different sources of data that can be obtained from these self-service interactions?

Product

Products have started to become increasingly electronic and therefore provide a large amount of data to the supplier concerning the product and its quality. In most cases, suppliers are also able to collect information about how consumers are using a certain product. Products can also provide the suppliers with information on the frequency of use of the product, any interruptions, or any other related aspects.

Electronic Touch Points

Organizations can collect a large amount of data just by using certain touchpoints that are used to shop for products. The IVR tree traversals are often logged, which meant Web clicks could be collected and so on and so forth.

Components

At times, components help to provide additional information, which includes data about the failures of components, their uses, or the lack of those uses. For instance, a wireless CSP would help in the collection of data from various networks, third parties, cell towers, or other handheld devices, which would help us to understand how components, when used together, would be good or bad for the customer.

Monetization

From the perspective of Big Data Analytics, it is possible to create a marketplace called a "data bazaar" where data can be collected and exchanged, as well as to help sell certain customer information. There is a new trend in the marketplace, in which the experience that certain customers have in one industry is anonymized, cleaned, packaged, and sometimes sold to other industries. Fortunately, Internet advertising helps to provide customers with an incentive to use services for free and certain opt-ins.

Internet advertising is a complex area. It has obtained a revenue of over $30 billion, which goes to show that the industry is feeding a large amount of information to start-ups and also helps organizations with their initial public offering (IPO) activities. The most interesting part is that this advertising money contributes to enhancing the experience that customers have. Consider Yelp for instance – this website lets consumers share the experiences they have when they visit restaurants, nightclubs, malls, and spas, and it also understands their likes and dislikes when it comes to life and so on. Yelp obtains its revenue through advertising on its website, but most of the traffic that the website receives is from people who read other customer experiences that have been posted on the website. With this traffic reaching the Internet, some questions arise on how the usage of the Internet to capture experiences would help improve revenue for other companies.

Big Data Analytics helps to create a new market, which would help customers obtain data from one industry and also use it in another to help improve an organization's ability to increase its revenue.

Location

It was discussed earlier that the area is critical to suppliers because that would help them reach their target audience with ease. If it is assumed that a particular product is used with a mobile device, the location of the consumer would be critical, and this information would be helpful to the supplier.

Cookie

Most browsers carry a large amount of data using cookies. Some of this information could be directly associated with touch points.

Usage Data

A lot of data providers have begun to collect, categorize, synthesize, and pack information that can be used in the future, too. This would usually include credit-rating agencies that rate their customers, social networks with blogs that have been liked, and certain cable companies that would have some audience information. Some or maybe most of the data could be anonymized or be provided only in summary form.

Big Data Applications

This section discusses different uses of Big Data Analytics. In each of the cases mentioned in this section, Big Data Analytics has started to integrate with business processes and certain traditional analytics practices, which help to provide the main outcomes. In most cases, the uses would represent the game changers that are essential to the growth and survival of any organization in a competitive marketplace. Some of these applications could are still in their infancy, but there are others that have become very common.

Social Media Command Center

In the year 2014, Blackberry faced a serious crisis when the email servers used were down for more than a day. Most people had tried to turn on and turn off their Blackberry devices because they were unaware of whether or not it was an issue with the device or whether it was the CSP. Most people would never have thought about how this problem could have occurred on the Blackberry server. When most consumers called the CSP, they realized that the CSP had absolutely no idea about the issue.

It is a known fact that the VP of Blackberry is often glued to Twitter, looking for any problems faced by customers. Often, a problem with the server is identified on Twitter before the Internal monitoring team can even process the issue. There are some employees who are a part of the customer service team, marketing team, or the public relations team whose job is to look through social media for information. This does sound like an automation opportunity.

A social media command center often combines the feedback from most consumers using automated search and display on different social media. The feedback is most often summarized in the form of "negative" or "positive" sentiments. When the feedback is obtained, the marketer can always respond to the comments by entering into a conversation with the consumers affected either positively or negatively and then deciding whether or not they would need to respond to the questions or obtain feedback on new products. Through these conversations, they will be able to obtain automated solutions that would help the organization. The automated solutions are great at helping the consumer find information, categorize it based on the attributes, and also organize that information on dashboards, thereby orchestrating responses from consumers in a fraction of a second.

Product Knowledge Hub

When consumers begin to turn into sophisticated users of products and technology, and the marketplace becomes a specialized area for customers, product knowledge would rarely belong to only one organization. If you consider the iPhone, you will notice that although the product is marketed by Apple, the parts for the phone come from different suppliers, while the apps come from a community of app developers, and the communication services are provided by a CSP. Android, created by Google, is more diverse. Google only provides the operating system, but the cell phone manufacturers offer the device. Smartphones can never work in isolation. They can also act as Wi-Fi hubs for some other devices. What would happen when you want to tether your iPhone to an iPad? Would you call Apple for help? Or would you reach out to your service provider? Or would the website provide all the information you need?

The answer to these questions is based on three sets of technologies. The first part of the answer lies with the capability to tap into any source of data that is found. Most CSPs have pieces of the solution on their intranet that is put together by customer service subject matter experts or product managers. Some of the information could also come from a third party or a device manufacturer. This data would need to be pulled together and stripped of its control information so that raw text could be reused.

The second part is to be able to categorize the raw information using a set of indices that are created by the product manager. This also implies that the information can be found whenever needed. Given that there are some combinations of products that are in existence, it is important for organizations to collect and combine the information that is often searched on devices. The indexing system would help to organize the information to make it easily accessible.

The final part of the solution would involve creating an XML document against certain queries that could be rendered or created using a mashup engine, or it could be made available to third-party applications.

What is created is a product knowledge hub that would now be used from a website or distributed to different call centers. This would significantly help to reduce the call handling time in call centers and would also contribute to increasing the number of solutions provided on the first call. When this information is freely available on the Internet, it helps to promote CSP websites as a source of knowledge, which would increase the traffic on the Web, thereby reducing the number of people who would contact the call center about any problems they may have.

When a single source of knowledge has been created, the source could be used to upsell some products and also connect the useful knowledge to certain product features, thereby enhancing the knowledge pool to help discover newer goods and render business partnership ideas. A lot of fragmented and stray knowledge about the products could be used to find a variety of other uses for the product.

Infrastructure and Operations Study

Numerous industries are exploring the use of Big Data to help to improve their analytical infrastructure. Most often, the best way to explore these improvements is by attempting to understand the utilization of the infrastructure and how bottlenecks or any other configurations would impact performance. In the past, most data were manually collected, and this significantly increased the cost to the organization. Big Data helps to provide a natural source of data without having to use people to collect the information by going from door to door.

Chapter 5

Introduction to Data Mining

Data mining is an analytical process that you can use for your business to convert raw data into relevant information that you can use. By using specialized tools, you can detect patterns in large-scale information to learn more about your customers and, in response, develop more effective strategies. The goal is to decrease your expenditures and increase your revenue. Effective data mining relies on efficient data gathering and storage, as well as analytical processing.

Retail shops, such as grocery stores and supermarkets, are the most common users of data mining. Many retailers are offering loyalty rewards, which enable their customers to buy items at reduced prices or accumulate points. The loyalty cards could make it easier for these businesses to monitor that is purchasing what, the time that they are shopping it, and at what price margin. After doing some analysis, the business could use this information for several purposes, such as providing customer coupons specifically targeted to their purchasing intent and deciding when to place items on sale or when to sell specific products at a higher markup.

Software

Software that is specially designed for data mining can analyze patterns and relationships in data according to the specifications requested by the business. For instance, data mining software could be used to develop classes of information. Let's say a grocery store likes to use data mining to identify the right time to offer certain products. It refers to the data it has captured and creates classes according to customer visits and what they have purchased. In some instances, data mining specialists may look for clusters of data according to logical relationships, or they study associations and patterns to make conclusions about consumer trends.

Strategies

Businesses can use different types of analyses to retrieve some valuable information from the data. Every type of business data analytics will have varying results or impacts. The type of data mining strategy you must use is dependent on the kind of business problem that you want to address.

Different forms of data analytics could result in different outcomes and thus offer different insights for the business. Among the most common ways to retrieve valuable insights is through the data mining process.

In developing your data analytics strategy, you must be clear on the definition of data mining and how it could help your business. You must remember that the most important goal of any process in data mining is to look for some relevant information that can be put in a database or warehouse. Let us look at some common types of data mining analytics that you can use for your business.

Association Analysis

Association analysis helps a business define and identify the associations between the numerous variables in the dataset. This data mining strategy helps you identify the concealed patterns in your data set. You can use these patterns to identify the variables and all the occurrence of other variables in the data set that exist in different frequencies.

This data analytics strategy is often used by retail stores to look for some patterns in the information from POS. These patterns can then be used to recommend some new products to customers depending on their previous purchases. If you do this correctly, you can ensure that your customer conversion rate increases.

In the year 2004, Walmart used data mining to understand the sales pattern for different products, especially the Strawberry pops. This retail giant realized that the sale of Strawberry Pops always increased before a hurricane. Walmart then began to place this product near the checkout counter whenever there was a hurricane striking the area.

Anomaly Detection

Anomaly detection is a type of data mining technique where you look for variables in a dataset that do not match a predicted pattern or expected behavior. These anomalies are often termed as surprises, outliers, exceptions, contaminants, or extremes. That said, these variables offer some important information about the data set. An outlier is an object that can deviate from the average or the standard deviation of the variables in the data set. Outliers are always separate from the other data you have in the dataset, which means that they can signify that there is some inconsistency in the data or that the engineer or user needs to analyze the numbers.

You can identify frauds in a system using anomalies in the data set. These variables will have a distinct set of characteristics that will help you determine the outcome of the data set. Businesses can use this method to identify those areas in their business where the processes are flawed. They can also use these methods to identify any fraud in the business. It is important to remember that in a large-scale data set, there will be a small number of anomalies. These variables may show some bad data, but these can also be present in the data set because of a variation in the data set. These variables can also show that there is something impressive about the data set. It is in these situations that you will need to perform more analysis.

Regression Analysis

You can identify the dependency of different variables or attributes in the data set using regression analysis. There is an assumption that one variable can affect the response of another variable. Independent attributes can be affected by another attribute, but this does not mean that there is some form or level of dependency. You, as a business owner, can identify whether the variables in the dataset are dependent on one another or not.

Regression analysis can help businesses identify the different levels of customer satisfaction or determine the number of clients the business has. Businesses can also use this analysis to see how a change in the business structure will affect customer loyalty. The business can also understand how the different service levels can be affected because of some external factors.

Every dating website uses regression analysis to offer better services to the members. Almost all websites use regression analysis to help two members connect based on their attributes. Tinder is a classic example, where you only receive notifications about people who have similar hobbies and habits.

Data mining and science can be used by businesses to identify the right information and focus on that information to develop models. These models can then be used to make projections on how people or systems will behave. You can build better models if you gather more data.

Classification Analysis

Classification analysis is a technique where you need to gather some relevant and crucial information about different variables and factors. This type of data mining analytics can help a business identify which data set it will need to use to perform further analysis. Businesses often use classification analysis against cluster analysis, since classifying the data is a pre-requisite for the clustering algorithm.

Email providers often use classification analysis to classify the email that any user receives as spam or useful. This can be done using data that is present in the email; for example, the algorithm can use the files attached in the email to define whether the email is useful or not.

Clustering Analysis

Clustering analysis is another data mining process that refers to the process of identifying the data sets that have some similar attributes and using those attributes to learn the similarities and differences in the data. Clusters have some specific traits, which an engineer can use to enhance the algorithm to improve targeting. For example, clusters of customer information that talks about customer purchasing behavior can be targeted to identify how the customer database would react to a change in products and services.

An outcome of clustering analysis is that you can develop some customer personas that you can identify a group of customers with. This will help you represent the customer types in a specific demographic. If you want to define these customer types, you should always look at customer attitude or behavior and also identify the customers who are using your products and services. The business can use a particular software or programming language to work on relevant cluster analysis.

Chapter 6

Introduction to Data Science

People across the world always collect data and use that data to do some analyses. In the past, it was difficult for people to collect data from devices like mobile phones and computers, but now, one can collect data from any device. Take smart watches as an example. You synchronize the smartwatch with your phone. This means that one can access the data on your phone through your watch. In other words, every interaction made on social media using files or pictures generates data. You also generate data when you look for some information on Google. Have you ever noticed that some advertisements pop up on your search page when you look for some information? If you pay close attention to these advertisements, you will notice that the products are similar to those that you were previously looking for or purchased.

The need to collect and use data, also called data immersion, is not a new phenomenon, but it is one that is accelerating at a rapid pace. The tiny puddles of data have become rivers and floods of data, and these data are available in different forms – structured, semi-structured, and unstructured. There are huge volumes of data that are being collected from every activity that is taking place across the globe.

You may wonder what the point of all this data is, and why we need to collect it. You may also wonder why we need to use resources to obtain this data. A few decades ago, people never worried about collecting data and using that data to make informed decisions. Today, the tides have turned, and data engineers across the globe are trying to identify different ways to capture, derive, collect, condense, and analyze the large volumes of data that are collected. Data scientists look for a way to derive some value from the data. They analyze the data and look for different ways to improve businesses and processes.

In its truest form, data science represents the process and resource optimization of data analysis. One can produce a variety of insights from data analysis, and these insights can be used to improve businesses, investments, lifestyles, health, and social life. You can use data science to help you understand and predict the route that you should take to achieve your goals. You can also look at what types of obstacles you may face on your way.

Who can make use of Data Science
The terms data science and data engineering are often misused and confused. You must remember that these fields are separate and distinct domains. We will look at data engineering in the following

chapters. Regardless of whether you are a data scientist or a data engineer, you will work with the following types of data:

Structured Data

Structured data is the data that are collected, collated, processed, manipulated, and analyzed using traditional relational databases.

Unstructured Data

Unstructured data are data that are generated through a variety of human activities. This data can be generated through pictures, files, texts, audio-visual files, and other types of data that cannot be categorized in a relational database.

Semi-structured data

Semi-structured data is the type of data that does not fit into any database system. This data, however, can be categorized using tags, which will help you create some hierarchy and order in the data.

Most people believe that only organizations with massive funding are implementing data science technologies and methodologies to improve and optimize their business, but this is not the case. The expansion of data has given rise to a demand for insights, and this demand has embedded itself in modern culture. The need for data insights and data has now become ubiquitous since organizations and firms of all sizes have begun to recognize the competitive environment; they are immersed in.

You may be wondering what this has to do with you. Firstly, you will need to understand that the culture has changed and you will need to keep up. This does not mean that you will need to go back to school and pursue a degree in computer science, data science, or statistics. The data revolution is not different from any other revolution that has hit the world. To stay relevant, you will need to take some time out to acquire and develop the skills that will help to keep you abreast of current developments. When it comes to learning about data science, you will only need to take up some courses online or read books like this one or attend events where you can learn whatever you need to stay on top of the game.

Who do you think can use data science? You can. Your firm can. Your employees can. Your employer can. Anyone who has even the least bit of training or understanding can use data insights to improve their business, lives, careers, and the well – being of their lives and businesses. Data science changes the way you approach the world. Most people use data insights to provide people with a vision to help them drive change and also make things happen. You can use these insights to bring about the following changes:

- Improve the effectiveness of marketing and sales initiatives
- Keep communities safer
- Optimize business systems
- Maximize the return on investment
- Make the world a better place for a the less fortunate

Chapter 7

Big Data Analytics versus Data Science versus Data Analytics

This chapter will cover some of the differences between data science, big data, and data analytics.

Data Analytics

Data analytics is the science of collecting and analyzing raw data to draw conclusions or analyses from that information. This field involves the application of a mechanical or algorithmic process which will help the analyst or user derive some insight from the data. For instance, you can run many data sets through a process that will help you identify a meaningful correlation between the datasets.

Data analytics is used in different fields and industries and allows companies and organizations to make informed decisions about their businesses. They can also use different tools to verify or disprove some existing models and theories. The focus of this type of science lies only in inference. The inference is the process of obtaining the conclusions based on the data and what the analyst knows.

Big Data

Big data refers to the massive volumes of data that you cannot process using traditional methods and applications that exist. When it comes to Big Data, you have to first start with the raw data that is not yet cleaned or collated. It is also impossible to store all that information on the computer because of the volume of the data.

From the previous chapter, you know that data can be collected from any device or person. This data can be structured, unstructured, and semi-structured, and the volume of this data overwhelms a business on a day-to-day basis. An analyst or business owner can use this data to analyze and derive insights from the data, which will lead to better strategic business moves and decisions. Gartner said that big data is high velocity, wide variety, and high-volume information that demands cost-effective and innovative forms of processing, which provide enhanced decision making, process automation, and insight.

Applications of Data Science, Data Analytics and Big Data

This section covers some of the applications of data science, data analytics, and big data.

Data Science

Internet Search

Most search engines use data science algorithms to deliver the best results when someone looks for a query in a nanosecond or less.

Digital Advertisements

Every organization, big or small, in the digital marketing industry, always uses some data science algorithm to develop digital billboards and display banners. It is for this reason that digital advertisements receive more responses when compared to traditional advertisements.

Recommender Systems

Recommender systems make it easy for an individual to find the right product from the massive volume of products available. These systems also improve user-experience. Many companies are using this system to promote and suggest their products, depending on what the user wants and demands. These suggestions are always based on the user's previous searches and purchases.

Big Data

Financial Services

Retail banks, credit card companies, insurance firms, private wealth management advisories, institutional investment banks, and venture funds always use big data for the financial services that they provide. The issue with these is that each of these organizations uses massive volumes of data that have many categories. Therefore, big data is used in the following ways:

- Compliance Analysis
- Customer Analysis
- Operational Analytics
- Fraud Analytics
- Communications

Retaining customers, gaining new subscribers, or expanding within the current base are the top priorities for most telecommunication service providers. The solutions to all these challenges lie only in the ability to analyze and combine the massive volumes of customer and machine-generated data, which is created every single day.

Retail

Regardless of whether you own a retail or online store, the only way you can stay in the game is by understanding what your customers want, and how you can serve them better. This will require you to have the ability to analyze different types of data from a variety of sources. These sources include customer transaction data, weblogs, social media, loyalty program data, and store-branded credit card data.

Data Analysis

Healthcare

Like every organization, a hospital also has issues with cost and always looks for ways to minimize cost. The challenge here is that the hospital must learn to cut or tighten costs while it treats the maximum number of patients and improves the quality of patient care. Hospitals now use machine and instrument data to optimize and track treatment, patient flow, and the equipment that the hospital uses. Experts have said that there will be a one percent gain in efficiency if hospitals continue to use this data. This means that hospitals can globally save $63 billion.

Travel

Through data analytics, companies can optimize and enhance the buying experience of their customers through the data they obtain from social media and weblog data analysis. Many travel sites try to gain insights into their customers' preferences and desires using data analytics. They can upsell their products by correlating user preferences with the current sales. They identify user preferences by following their customer's browsing. This allows companies to create customized offers and packages.

Gaming

Companies developing games can collect the following data and use that data to optimize and enhance the user experience within the game:

- Likes and dislikes of the customer

- What types of games do customers prefer buying?
- Relationships that the customer shares with characters in the game

Energy Management

Firms use data analytics to manage the consumption of energy. This includes energy optimization, smart-grid management, building automation, and energy distribution in utility companies. The applications or algorithms are centered upon the monitoring and control of dispatch crews, manage service outages and network devices. An engineer can use the millions of data points present in the utility network and monitor the use of energy.

Skills Required

Data Science and Data Analytics

Programming Languages

Regardless of what role you are interviewing for, you are expected to learn to use some statistical programming languages like Python, R, and query languages like SQL. These are important to know since they are considered the tools of the trade.

Statistics

You must have a good understanding of the subject. You must be aware of the different tests, methods, distributions, probability, and maximum likelihood estimators. You must know these concepts well since they will help you understand and analyze data better. The trick is to identifying the right method to use for different data sets. Data-driven companies use statistics to understand their customers and also to make decisions that will benefit the company.

Machine Learning

If you work in a large company that uses big data or large volumes of data or is working at a data-driven company like Uber, Google Maps, and Netflix, you must understand what machine learning is and its different learning methods. Most techniques that are implemented to help a machine learn can be implemented using Python or R. Therefore, and it does not necessarily mean that you need to know how the algorithms work. It is important to understand what machine learning is at a broad level.

Linear Algebra and Multivariate Calculus

One must understand these concepts, especially if you are working in a company that is defined by data since any improvement made to the algorithm will help in predicting outcomes that will help in improving the status of the company. You may be asked to derive or obtain some results using statistical methods during the interview. You may wonder why a data scientist will have to understand these concepts when one can use R or Python for the same. The answer is that it is best to learn these concepts so a data scientist can implement these concepts in their work without having to use R or Python.

Data Wrangling

The data that is being analyzed is often difficult to work with and can be messy. Therefore, it becomes important to know how one can deal with any imperfection in the data. These imperfections are important to note, and it is important to master this skill regardless of which company you are working for.

Data Communication and Visualization

It is important for you to build this skill, especially if you own or work for a young company, which uses data to make decisions for the future. This skill is also useful in companies where the data scientist is viewed as a person who helps the company and other employees of the company make informed decisions. Concerning communication, you will need to represent your findings and also describe it to a large audience. You can use visual aids like graphs and charts to enhance your communication.

Software Engineering

If you are being interviewed for a new company, and are the first data scientist to be interviewed, it is important that you learn some software and also learn how to build code. It is important since you will be working on developing new products.

Data Intuition

Companies always want to know if you are someone who can solve problems. You have to think of how you will be working with data engineers, product managers, and employees to understand data. You must use your intuition to understand what will need to be done with the data to obtain the solution.

Big Data

Analytical Skills

You must have the ability to make sense of the volumes of data that you have and work with. You should also ensure that you use your analytical skills to identify a relevant solution to a problem.

Creativity

You must have the ability to create and develop new methods that will help you interpret, collect, and analyze any strategy. This skill is important for one to possess.

Business Skills

Every big data professional must understand business objectives and the processes that drive the growth of the business.

Apart from these skills, a big data professional must also know mathematics and statistics and should be well-versed in some programming languages.

Tips and Tricks

Now that we know what data science, data analytics, and big data are, let us look at some tips that will help you make it in the world of data science. This section gives you some pointers and also helps you understand how to face interviews and when the right time is to jump to a different company.

- Learn how to clean and munge the data. The latter is a process that converts raw data to a format that is easy for the data scientist, analyst, or big data professionals to analyze. The former is a method that is used to remove duplication and data that hampers the analysis. These tools are essential for a data scientist, analyst, or big data professional to possess.

- Brush up on your statistics and mathematics skills as a data scientist, analyst, or big data professional, analyst, and big data professionals must know what the data is trying to tell them. To do that, you will need to understand statistics and probability. You may need to learn advanced mathematics for some positions, but this is the best place to start.

- When you want to become a data scientist, analyst, or big data professional, there are some steps that you will need to follow to ensure that you achieve your aim.

- Learn how to code. Data scientists, analysts, or big data professionals need to learn languages like R and Python to teach the computer to analyze data.

- Follow the leaders in the data science industry and read their blogs to understand and learn more about data science. This will help you stay abreast of new theories.

- Understand what databases are and how data can be stored. It is important to understand how databases are built since it is important to learn how to build those repositories. This will help you identify the big picture.

- Understand what machine learning is and the different types of learning like supervised, unsupervised, and reinforcement learning.

- Gain expertise and learn more tools only once you have mastered the skills above. It would be best to learn other programming languages and also learn new ways to analyze data. It is this extra learning that will set you apart from your competitors.
- You must practice how to use data science to analyze and interpret data. You can do this by developing your data source and work with other data scientists, analysts, or big data professionals. It is always better to have some work that you can show to your interviewer.
- Understand how important it is to visualize and report data. You do not have to become a graphic designer, but you must understand how to create reports that a layman will understand.

Chapter 8

Data Visualization

Through data visualization, one can explain the significance of the data using visual aids like graphs and charts. Trends, correlations, and patterns are often undetected in text-based summaries. Therefore, it is always a good idea to use data visualization techniques to understand the significance of the data. Today, the tools that one can use to depict data go beyond the standard graphs and charts that one uses in an Excel spreadsheet. You can display the data using infographics, gauges, and dials, spark lines, geographic maps, fever charts, detailed pie and bar charts, and heat maps. The images can include interactive capabilities that will allow the users to drill or manipulate the data in the images to analyze the information.

Importance of data visualization

A data visualization tool is important since it is easier to operate when compared to the early versions of business intelligence software or traditional statistical analysis software.

Data visualization tools and software play a crucial role in advanced analytics and big data projects. When businesses accumulate massive volumes of data, they need to identify a way to understand and interpret that data in an easy way. Therefore, businesses began to prefer visualization tools.

It is for the same reason that visualization is important. When a data scientist writes advanced machine learning or predictive analytics algorithms, he or she needs to visualize the output of the algorithm. This will allow the scientist to monitor the results and ensure that models perform as intended.

Examples of data visualization

You can use data visualization tools in different ways. The most common use of visualization tools is BI reporting. A user can set up different visualization tools that will allow him or her to generate an automatic dashboard that will track the performance of the company. The user can also define the performance indicators and allow the tool to interpret the results.

Different departments in a business implement data visualization software. These tools allow the departments to track their work and initiatives. For instance, the marketing team may want to implement software that will monitor the performance of an email campaign. They may want to track the conversion rate, the click-through rate, and the open rate.

Data visualization vendors extend the functionality of the tools, and these tools are being used as the front end for big data environments. In these environments, data visualization tools help data scientists and engineers track the data sources and perform some exploratory analysis on the data before they perform extensive analysis.

How data visualization works

The tools used for data visualization come with different connectors that allow you to populate the data from a variety of sources. These sources include cloud storage platforms, Hadoop, and relational databases. The visualization software will pull the data in from these courses and then apply a graphic type to that data as per your choice.

Data visualization software also allows the user to define how they want to present the data. Now, the development of software has automated this step. Some tools interpret the shape that the chart has to take and identifies the correlations between the variables in the data. It will then use this analysis to visualize the data.

Every data visualization software allows users to source a variety of analyses into a single page using a dashboard component. These dashboards are often a web portal.

Chapter 9

Data Integration

Data integration refers to the process of combining data from independent sources, which are warehoused using different tools and usually offer a single perspective of data. Integrating data is crucial in the case of merging two businesses or consolidating systems inside one company to get a single aspect of the data assets of the company.

Probably the most common step in data integration is to set up the data warehouse. The advantage of a data warehouse is that it will enable a business to conduct analyses according to the data inside the warehouse. This may not be doable on data available on different source systems because such systems may not have the required data, although the data sets may be named similarly.

Moreover, if you want to keep data integration solutions completely aligned with your business goals, then you have to be mindful of the particular kinds of business value that could result from the efficient use of tools and strategies for integrating data.

In this chapter, we will discuss the top ways that data integration can bring value to your business. There are several actual cases included in this chapter to show the various types of values that data integration can provide. Hopefully, this can help you explain to your partners or your boss the value of data integration. It could also serve you as a guide on how you can plan and design suitable data integration strategies to advance your business.

Value

Let us begin with a more generalized perspective of data integration. Most valuable data-driven practices in business often rely on one or several forms of data integration. There are business processes that cannot be functional without data integration. This is particularly true for data warehousing and business intelligence.

Remember, effective decisions may rely on calculated, aggregated, and time-bounded data sets within a data warehouse, and this can never take place without effective data integration. Success in sales, for example, usually relies on a total view of every customer's information that is usually aggregated using tools and techniques for data integration.

Moreover, integrating various businesses, as well as their processes, using shared data, should be backed up by a data integration solution. This is helpful, whether the businesses are divisions inside one enterprise or different enterprises that can share data from one business to another. Meanwhile, business processes like just-in-time inventory or operational business intelligence should be backed up by an efficient data integration solution, which could be used in real-time or with a few delays.

As you try to advance your business, your pace will also accelerate. Data integration could speed up the process of gathering and integrating time-sensitive data at speeds that are not even possible a decade ago. Data integration and related business processes, such as data management and data quality assurance, can add value to business data. As a result, the value of business processes will also increase.

Identifying the Value of Data Integration

Identifying the business value of data integration once you see it can be more difficult than you might expect because this data analytics process is usually separated at a level or two from the systems that your business might be using. Nevertheless, in general, the data integration value is usually visible as valuable data. Below are common examples of data integration in this value field:

- A business executive who accesses a single view of customer information that was built with data integration through data sync.
- A business intelligence user enters a query into a data warehouse, after which the system responded with complete data models and metadata that were set up using data integration.

- Several business supervisors are accessing information on a computer that is updated in real-time or as needed through a data integration solution.
- A product supervisor who accesses a list of available supplies from a supplier within a data set, which the supplier established through data integration and delivered across business boundaries through the business-to-business exchange.

Even if data is accessible in a Graphical User Interface (GUI) or a report, business users may overlook that data integration provided the information. Many business executives fail to realize that data integration is responsible for collecting, preparing, and delivering most of the data that they may take for granted. Nowadays, data integration is a fast-changing discipline, which offers data for several types of applications, whether they are operational or analytical.

Benefits

The outcome of data integration is quite ubiquitous in the business world, which enables commercial activities. We often don't identify these activities to consider data integration as a crucial process in today's business.

If your business needs to confirm the value of data integration (a common requirement for sponsorship, investment, or approval for data integration), then you have to educate your partners or your boss about the critical role that data integration could play for your data-driven business processes.

Single, Unified View of Business Entities

Through data integration, the business can capture data from several sources to complete a single view of the entities of the business, such as assets, locations, staff, finances, products, and clients. This is on the same level of data warehousing, but this is more on operations and not on business intelligence.

By effectively using data integration, the business can complete its customer profile and improve value for any client-oriented business process, from sales and marketing to client support. Complete product data can also add value to business systems for procurement, product management, and supply chain manufacturing.

Data Warehousing and Business Intelligence

As a support system of data warehousing, data integration can add value to the business process. Through data integration, you can collect raw data from different sources and combine them to develop new products. A data warehouse will contain data and data sets that do not exist anywhere else in the business.

Moreover, because of the requirements of business intelligence, data that goes into the warehouse should be regularly reconfigured to develop calculated, aggregated, and time-bounded data, established into multichannel data sets. Data integration cannot collect data itself; rather, it can shift the data into these necessary structures.

Data integration for business intelligence will allow high-value processes. A data warehouse constructed through data integration allows decision making at the tactical, strategic, and operational layers. Data created through data integration is crucial to business intelligence strategies, such as dashboard reporting, performance management, advanced analytics, and online analytics. These data warehousing and business intelligence activities – also enabled by data integration – could help in customer retention, increase sales, improve the efficiency of business operations, guide sales, and marketing activities, enable strategic planning, and other valuable business outcomes.

Real-time Delivery of Data
Businesses need to adapt to the fast pace of the world, and data integration can help in integrating data at speeds that were impossible a decade ago. Real-time data delivery that is usually enabled by modern data integration systems can enable several high-value business processes.

Businesses are now using applications to monitor data, such as business activities, facility status, grid monitoring, and so on. These can be quite impossible without the real-time capacity for information delivery supported by data integration.

Operational business intelligence often captures data several times a day from operational applications and makes the data available for monitoring and other kinds of management or operational reports. This provides the business access to data for strategic and operational decision-making.

Data Integration Could Add Value to Business Data

Many business owners think of data integration as a process of moving data. Those who are trained in data science understand that it is not easy to just move data around. There is a need to improve it. Every ideal data integration solution can add value to the process.

Data integration improves data during the process. Data quality strategies are being added to data integration solutions. This is organic because data integration could filter out concerns about data quality that should be fixed, as well as areas for improvement. Data integration can also help in improving metadata, data models, master data, and other attributes of data. Hence, the data could come out as complete, clean, and consistent.

Data integration can also help in building new databases that are valuable for the business. Remember that the data contained in the data warehouse can never be found anywhere else in the business. Similar to the value-adding system in manufacturing, data integration can capture raw materials and build them into new data sets.

Therefore, data integration can convert data to make it more valuable for more business processes. Aside from moving data, data integration can also convert data, so it is suitable for any target system. In simple words, data integration repurposes data, so more business units, as well as their processes, could be beneficial for the business.

Data Replication

Data replication, also known as data synchronization, is another data integration system that can help add value to any business. For instance, data replication may build a complete view of a central data hub for access by several users and applications. This is seen in central hubs for product data, customer data, and master data. Replication may also enhance relevant data across several applications, along with their databases. For instance, client-facing applications for contact centers can be limited to a partial view of a customer, unless a total view can be developed by replicating customer data across these applications.

Data's business value in replication is that more business owners have a more unified view of a separate entity, such as finances, customers, and products. Nevertheless, data replication systems may tend to move and integrate data more often – usually several times a day. This hastens the freshness or data currency in applications. Hence, data is not just complete but also updated, which is crucial for businesses that need current data for their decision-making.

B2B Data Exchange

B2B data exchange is a promising area for development because businesses can use data integration tools and strategies in areas where these could be rare. Many data exchanges are low-tech and manually entered, which should be replaced to be synchronized. Experts project a wide modernization in data exchange between businesses, especially in product-centric enterprises like retail, suppliers, and manufacturing. This is also crucial for financial institutions, healthcare, and other organizations that are using procurement and supply chain systems.

The need to modernize data exchange between businesses is an urgent concern. There is also a need to develop business value in this area. In general, business partnerships are crucial to advance businesses in terms of market reach, revenue, and brand development. Business partnerships can grow by achieving better operational excellence through data integration.

Collaborative Practices

To ensure that data integration offers the best type of business value, the system must be aligned with the goals of the business that is relative to the data. Fortunately, several collaborative practices have emerged in recent years, so data specialists could easily streamline their work with a broad range of colleagues.

Collaborative Data Integration

Collaborative data integration is a loose strategy for coordinating the tasks of data integration teams, which include data specialists. In general, collaborative data integration uses applications and practices like code review, team hierarchy, project management, and software versioning.

Data Governance

Data governance refers to data integration processes that focus on privacy, security, risk, and compliance. Many businesses have expanded data governance to also cover quality, standards, architecture, and many other issues on data. The team working on data governance could help data scientists get a single view of business goals that are relevant to data and align their work properly. Meanwhile, the change management process of data integration can enable data integration specialists to think of possible solutions to increase data value.

Unified Data Management

Unified data management is a recent business practice that aims to coordinate tasks across several data management disciplines described above. UDM also enables collaboration between business management and data management to ensure that most data management tasks add business value by supporting business management goals.

Data Stewardship

Data stewardship is designed for managing the quality of data by identifying and prioritizing the quality of work according to the needs of the business and certain parameters, such as technological capacity and budget. The person who is in charge of the data, also known as the data steward, should work together with business and technical people. Through the years, data integration specialists have used stewardship in their array of strategies for better credibility in the alignment and prioritization of data integration work.

Chapter 10

Best Algorithms for Analytics

A s mentioned previously, this chapter consists of a few algorithms for analytics that will enhance the results you obtain. These algorithms make your life easier by helping you obtain the results in the simplest form with you having to do either minimal or no work at all.

Support vector machines

What does it do?
Support vector machines are a little complicated to understand. These algorithms work towards trying to classify data into two classes using hyperplanes. This algorithm performs a function similar to C4.5, but it does not use any decision trees. Now, what are hyperplanes? A hyperplane is a function written exactly like the line of an equation. If you have to classify data based only on two features, you will find that the hyperplane is, in fact, a line.

It is a fact that the support vector machines can ensure that they project your data into dimensions of a higher level. When the data has been projected to a higher level, the support vector machine tries to identify the right hyperplane to classify your data into two classes.

Let us consider an extremely simple example. There are milk chocolates and dark chocolates on the table. If the chocolates have not been mixed around, you will be able to differentiate between the chocolates. As they have not been separated, you will need to sit down and read the name on each one and then separate them.

When you place a bar of new chocolate on the table, you will know exactly where the chocolate needs to go without needing to predict the color. The chocolates here represent the data points, the milk chocolate and dark chocolate represent the classes of data, and your hands represent the hyperplane that is, in fact, a line.

The support vector machine works out which hyperplane suits the data the best. What should you do when things have gone wrong? Things may go wrong, and they often do. If the chocolates have not been mixed, then there is no point in using your hands to separate them. Let us look at how you can work on the same.

Now, lift all the chocolates into the air and then divide the chocolates when they are in the air itself. When you move the chocolates around, you will be able to map your data into dimensions at a higher level. You will now have moved from two-dimensional space to a three-dimensional space. How does the algorithm do this? The algorithm is based on mathematical functions where the kernel of the function is used to depict the higher dimensions.

C4.5

What does it do?

This algorithm needs data that has already been classified. The algorithm works towards constructing a new way of classifying the data using a decision tree. It is for this reason that the data must be classified.

The C4.5 creates a classifier when it is looking for a way to classify the data into a decision tree. So what is this classifier? It is a tool that works towards analyzing which group or category the new set of data constitutes.

Let us consider an example of a set of students in a classroom. You know how well the students perform. You also know their strengths and weaknesses and how they behave in class. This information is called the attribute of the student. Now, you want to use all these attributes to gather information on the number of students who will successfully graduate this year. This algorithm uses the data that it has on each student and creates a decision tree that will help you obtain the final decision. Now, what are decision trees?

A decision tree is a flowchart that will help you classify new data. The advantage of a decision tree is that you can create different events that may involve the same person. Let us use the same example above:

1. A Student will graduate

2. A student has a high chance of graduating

3. The student is extremely distracted

4. The student will not graduate

At each of the points mentioned above, the algorithm will try to assign a value to the student and will provide you with the decision tree, thereby giving you the answer you need.

Why should you use this software when you can make the decision tree on your own? You may make an error. With the algorithm, there is no chance of an error, and you will be able to read the final data with ease.

AdaBoost

What does it do?

AdaBoost or Adaptive Boosting is a Meta – algorithm that is often used in machine learning and was formulated by Robert Schapire and Yoav Freund. This algorithm, like the CART algorithm, can be used in conjunction with various other algorithms to enhance their performance.

The output obtained from other algorithms, weak learners, is accumulated into a weighted sum that would represent the final output of the weighted or boosted variable or classifier. AdaBoost is an adaptive algorithm in the sense that the successive weak learners are tweaked to overcome any of the errors or misclassifications made by any other previous classifier.

In this algorithm, different learners are combined to create the final model, which provides the user with the predicted values or classifiers. Some of these learners could be weaker than others, but if all the errors of the individual learners are handled, the final model created would be very strong.

The algorithm is said to be adaptive since it continuously learns. The final algorithm obtained is called the learning algorithm, which continues to adapt depending on the problem at hand. Each learning algorithm is different from the other and is suitable for some problem types alone. These algorithms will have different configurations and parameters, which would need to be adjusted to achieve optimal performance on a particular dataset.

AdaBoost is referred to as one of the best classifiers. The main disadvantage of AdaBoost is that this algorithm is susceptible to changes that occur due to outliers and noisy data.

CART

What does it do?

Decision trees are often used in data mining to create a model that will help to predict the value of a target or dependent variable. This value is calculated using the values of other input variables that may or may not be dependent on each other. The CART Algorithm or Classification and Regression Trees Algorithm used decision trees to predict values and was introduced by Jerome Friedman, Richard Olshen, Charles Stone, and Leo Breiman in 1984. It uses two types of decision trees:

Classification Trees

These types of decision trees are used when the target variable is categorical, and the tree is often used to classify the target variable.

Regression Trees

These decision trees are used when the target variable is continuous. This tree helps to predict the values of the target variable.

The CART algorithm is a sequence of questions. The answers to the said questions are what determine the next questions that should follow if any. The answers to every question in the sequence form a tree-like structure where the end is a terminal node, after which there are no questions.

The main elements of a CART algorithm are as follows:

- Rules to split the data at every node based on the answers to questions or the value of the variable
- Rules to stop the tree when there is a terminal branch or if the answers cannot be split further
- A prediction for the target variable at every terminal node
  There are some features of CART that make it the easiest algorithm to use. There are a few cons when it comes to this particular algorithm.

- CART is a non – parametric algorithm and hence does not require the user to have any prior knowledge of different distributions that could be used
- Outliers in the data and input variables do not affect the algorithm
- The user can always reduce the size of the decision tree and relax the rules that are around certain questions. This approach reduces the probability of overlooking important values in the data by terminating the tree too soon.
- The CART algorithm uses both testing and cross-validation to verify if the data has been fitted correctly or not.
- The algorithm uses one variable multiple times in the decision tree, which makes it complex to uncover interdependencies that may exist between different sets of data.
- A user can use this algorithm along with other algorithms to select the set of input variables.

K–Means

The algorithm mentioned above uses the process of identifying a classifier. This algorithm uses clustering as the central idea.

What does it do?

This is an extremely popular cluster analysis technique that helps in the exploration of a dataset. This algorithm creates groups of clusters, all the members of which are similar in some way.

Let us consider the example that has been mentioned above. You have the data on every student, which can now be written as a vector. Now that you have created a vector, you are probably wondering how it is that K–Means will solve the rest for you. You should develop the vector, and K–Means does the rest. You may be wondering how it does the rest. Let us look at the section below.

1. K–Means will pick up the points in the multidimensional space that represent each of the clusters. These points are called the centroids.

2. Each student is close to at least one of the centroids that have been created. You will need to be hopeful of the fact that each student is not close to the same point but to different centroids in the space to ensure that the students form clusters.

3. Once you have obtained the clusters, you will know for a fact that each student is a member of one cluster only.

4. The algorithm works towards identifying the center of the clusters using the members of the clusters or the student vectors.

5. The center has now become the centroid of the cluster. Given that the centroid has moved, the cluster may also shift.

6. The process will continue to repeat until the centroid remains the same. This process is called convergence.

Why has K–Means gained immense popularity? It is because it is an extremely simple algorithm and has always worked faster than any other algorithm that has ever been made. It is also very efficient, even over very large datasets, since this algorithm will continue to cluster the big data around a centroid to look through the relationships between the data.

PageRank

What does it do?

PageRank is an algorithm that allows users to understand the importance of any website that appears on the Google search page. According to Google, this algorithm works by counting the quality and number of links that show up on a search engine page to estimate the importance of that website. It is based on the assumption that very important websites receive a lot more links from underlying websites.

Chapter 11

Data Mining Models

Different models can be used for data mining. These models revolve around certain topics from statistics, such as linear regression, ANOVA, least-square estimates, and various other topics. This section covers certain models that would make data mining easy for businesses and other users.

Dimension Reduction Methods

The databases that are used have thousands and millions of records and variables. It would be impossible to conclude that these variables are not dependent on one another with absolutely no correlation among them. A data user needs to keep in mind that there could be multiple collinearities between the variables. Multicollinearity is a phenomenon where predictor variables are all correlated in one way or another.

A lot of instability arises in the solution set when there is multicollinearity between variables. This will lead to incoherent results. For instance, if you look at multiple regression, you will find that multiple correlations between predictor variables will result in a solution that will have a significant impact on the solution set. This will hold true even if none of the variables have any significant impact on the solution set when considered independently.

Even if one were to identify a way to avoid such instability, if the user were to include variables that have a high level of correlation between them, this would lead to overemphasis on specific components of the model. This phenomenon occurs since this particular component is being counted twice.

When too many predictor variables are used, there is an unnecessary complication that arises when we need to identify the way to model a relationship between a response variable and the predictor variables. This will also complicate the analysis and its interpretation, and it also violates the principle of parsimony. The principle states that an analyst should always stick to a certain number of predictor variables, which will make it easy to interpret the analysis. If one were to retain too many variables, there is a possibility that there could be over fitting, which would lead to a hindrance in the analysis. The new data set will not behave in the same way as the training data that was used.

There is a possibility that the analysis performed could miss the relationship that exists between the predictors. For instance, there could be numerous single predictor variables that would fall into a single group or component that would address only one aspect of the data. If you were to look at a person's account, you would need to group the account balance and any deposits or savings made from that particular account into one category alone.

There are certain applications, such as image analysis, in which retaining the full dimensionality of the variable would make the problem at hand intractable. For instance, a face classification system based on 256×256 pixel images could potentially require vectors of dimension 65,536. Human beings can discern and understand certain patterns in an image at a glance; these patterns could elude the human eye if they were to be represented algebraically or graphically. The most advanced visualization techniques also do not go beyond five dimensions. How do you think we will be able to identify the relationships that could exist between a massive data set that has thousands of variables?

The goal of dimension reduction methods is to use the structure of correlation among the different predictor variables to accomplish the following goals:

- Reduce the number of predictor components in the data set
- Ensure that these predictor components are independent of one another
- Provide a dynamic framework which would help in the interpretation of the analysis

The most common dimension reduction methods are Principal Component Analysis (PCA), User Defined Composites, and Factor Analysis.

Regression Modeling

Regression modeling is an elegant and powerful method for estimating the value of continuous target variables. Multiple regression models could be used – one of the simplest models is the simple linear regression model. In this model, the relationship between a single continuous predictor variable and a single continuous response variable is represented using a straight line. There are also multiple regression models where numerous predictor variables can be used to estimate one response.

Apart from the methods mentioned above, there is also the least squared regression method that can be used to identify the relationship. That said, there is a certain level of disparity when it comes to the assumptions of the model. These assumptions must be validated before the model is even built. If the user were to build and use a model that was based on assumptions that have not been verified, this would lead to failures that could cause too much damage to the company or the individual.

Once the user has obtained the results from the model, he or she will need to be certain that there exists absolutely no linear relationship between the variables used in the model. There could be a relationship that exists that would be very granular and difficult to identify. There is, however, a systematic approach to determining whether there is any linear relationship between the variables, and that is using inference. Four inferential methods could be used to determine the relationship:

- The t-test is used to identify the relationship that exists between the predictor and response variables
- $\beta 1$, which defines the confidence interval for the slope
- The confidence interval that contains the values that the mean of the response variable can take depending on the value of the predictor variable
- Based on a specific value of the predictor, the interval of values that the response variable can take

The inferential methods described above all depend on the adherence of data to the assumptions that are made at the beginning of the process. The level at which the data adheres to the assumptions can be identified using two graphical methods – a plot of the normal probability and a plot of the standardized residuals against the predicted or fitted values.

The validity of the assumptions made in a regression model can be evaluated by identifying some patterns in the plot of the residuals versus the fit. If there are any patterns in the plot, it means that an assumption has been violated. Otherwise, the assumptions have adhered to word for word. You can apply the transformation assumptions, like the natural log transformation, to the response variable to remove any violations. You can also use the transformation functions, like the Box-Cox transformation or Mosteller and Tukey's ladder of re-expression, if there is a non-linear relationship between the predictor and response variables.

Multiple Regression

The previous section covered the process of linear regression. Let us now look at regression modeling using simple linear regression where we considered a single predictor variable and a single response variable. The only interest that data miners have is on the relationship that exists between multiple predictor variables and the target or response variable. Most applications built for data mining have a lot of data, with some sets including thousands or millions of variables, of which most have a linear relationship with the response or target variable. That is where a data miner would prefer to use a multiple linear regression model. These models provide improved accuracy and precision of prediction and estimation, similar to the improved accuracy of regression estimates over bivariate or univariate estimates.

Multiple linear regression models use linear surfaces like hyperplanes or planes to determine the relationship between a set of predictor variables and one continuous target or response variable. Predictor variables are often continuous, but there could be categorical predictor variables included in the model through the use of dummy or indicator variables. In a simple linear regression model, a straight line of dimension one is used to estimate the relationship between one predictor and the response variable. If we were to evaluate the relationship between two predictor variables and one response variable, we would have to use a plane to estimate it because a plane is a linear surface in two dimensions.

Regression with Categorical Predictors

So far, we have looked at regression models where the predictor variable follows a continuous distribution. You can also use a categorical predictor variable as an input in a regression model. You can do this by using a dummy or indicator variable. To do this, you must divide a variable with k categories into a set of k-1 variables. Indicator variables or dummy variables are binary variables, and these variables take the value zero if the value does not belong to the selected category and one otherwise.

Logistic Regression

Linear regression is used to define the relationship between a set of predictor variables and a continuous response variable. The response variable, however, is often categorical. In these cases, you cannot use linear regression but will need to use logistic regression, which is an analogous method. This method is like linear regression, but it allows you to establish the relationship between a set of predictor variables and a categorical response variable.

One of the most attractive properties of linear regression is that closed-form solutions for the optimal values of the regression coefficients may be obtained through the least-squares method. You can, however, not calculate closed-form solutions for these equations. You can find the maximum likelihood estimators by differentiating the likelihood function, $L(\beta|x)$, with respect to each parameter and then setting the resulting forms to be equal to zero. Therefore, other methods, such as iterative weighted least squares, must be applied.

In simple words, you can use linear regression to identify and assess the relationship between a set of predictor variables and a response variable. You can use logistic regression to identify and assess the relationship between a set of predictor variables and a categorical response variable. In logistic regression, it is assumed that there is a non-linear relationship between the predictor variables and the response variable. In linear regression, however, the response variable is a continuous random variable $Y = \beta0 + \beta1x + \varepsilon$ where the conditional mean is $\pi(x) = E(Y|x) = \beta0 + \beta1x$. The form of the conditional mean calculated in a logistic regression algorithm is different from the form calculated in a linear regression model.

Variable Selection Methods
You can use the variable selection methods to choose those variables that can be included in regression analysis. These selection methods are algorithms that can be used to develop the model using an optimal set of predictor variables.

Forward Selection Procedure
No variables are used in the model when employing this method.

Step 1: For the first variable to enter the model, select the predictor most highly correlated with the target. (Without loss of generality, denote this variable x1.) If the resulting model is not significant, stop and report that no variables are significant predictors; otherwise, proceed to step 2.

Step 2: For each remaining variable, compute the sequential F-statistic for that variable, given the variables already in the model. For example, in this first pass through the algorithm, these sequential F-statistics would be $F(x2|x1)$, $F(x3|x1)$, and $F(x4|x1)$. On the second pass through the algorithm, these might be $F(x3|x1, x2)$, and $F(x4|x1, x2)$. Select the variable with the largest sequential F-statistic.

Step 3: For the variable selected in step 2, test for the significance of the sequential F-statistic. If the resulting model is not significant, stop, and report the current model without adding the variable from step 2. Otherwise, add the variable from step 2 into the model, and return to step 2.

Backward Elimination Procedure

The backward elimination procedure begins with all the variables or all of a user-specified set of variables in the model.

Step 1: Perform the regression on the full model - that is, using all available variables. For example, perhaps the full model has four variables, namely, x1, x2, x3, and x4.

Step 2: For each variable in the current model, compute the partial F-statistic. In the first pass through the algorithm, these would be $F(x1|x2, x3, x4)$, $F(x2|x1, x3, x4)$, $F(x3|x1, x2, x4)$, and $F(x4|x1, x2, x3)$. Select the variable with the smallest partial F-statistic. Denote this value as F-min.

Step 3: Test for the significance of F-min. If F-min is not significant, remove the variable associated with F-min from the model, and return to step 2. If F-min is significant, stop the algorithm, and report the current model. If this is the first pass through the algorithm, the current model is the full model. If this is not the first pass, the current model has been reduced by one or more variables from the full model.

Stepwise Procedure

The stepwise procedure represents a modification of the forward selection procedure. A variable that has been entered into the model early in the forward selection process may turn out to be nonsignificant once other variables have been entered into the model. The stepwise procedure checks on this possibility by performing at each step a partial F-test using the partial sum of squares for each variable currently in the model. If there is a variable in the model that is no longer significant, the variable with the smallest partial F-statistic is removed from the model. The procedure terminates when no further variables can be entered or removed.

Best Subsets Procedure

For data sets where the number of predictors is not too large, the best subsets procedure represents an attractive variable selection method. If there are more than 30 or so predictors, the best subsets method encounters a combinatorial explosion and becomes intractably slow. The best subsets procedure works as follows:

Step 1: The analyst specifies how many (k) models of each size he or she would like to have reported, as well as the maximum number of predictors (p) the analyst wants in the model.

Step 2: All models of one predictor are built: for example, $y = \beta0 +\beta1$ (sugars) $+\varepsilon$, $y = \beta0 +\beta2$ (fiber)$+\varepsilon$, and so on. Their R2, R2adj, Mallows' Cp, and s values are calculated. The best k models are reported based on these measures.

Step 3: All models of the two predictors are built: for example, $y = \beta0 +\beta1$ (sugars) $+\beta2$(fiber)$+\varepsilon$, $y = \beta0 +\beta1$ (sugars)$+\beta4$(shelf2)$+\varepsilon$, and so on. Their R2, R2adj, Mallows' Cp, and s values are calculated, and the best k models are reported.

The procedure continues in this way until the maximum number of predictors (p) is reached. The analyst then has a listing of the best models of each size 1, 2... p to assist in the selection of the best overall model.

Naïve Bayes Estimation and Bayesian Networks

In the field of statistics, the probability is approached in two ways – the classical approach or the Bayesian approach. Probability is often taught using the classical approach or the frequentist approach. This is a method that is followed in all beginner's classes in statistics. In the frequentist approach to probability, the population parameters are fixed constants with values that are unknown. These prospects are defined to be "*the relative frequencies of the various categories, where the experiment is repeated an indefinitely large number of times."* For example, if we toss a coin ten times, the probability that we will obtain heads eight times out of ten is not unusual. If we toss the same coin 10 trillion times, the probability of us obtaining heads is approximately 50%. It is this behavior that defines the prospect of the frequentist approach.

Certain situations do arise in which the classical definition of probability makes it difficult to understand the situation. For example, how will you calculate the probability that there will be a terrorist attack in New York City? Given that such an occurrence has never occurred, it is difficult to conceive what the long-term behavior of this gruesome experiment might be. Another approach to probability, the frequentist approach, uses parameters that are fixed so that the randomness lies only in the data. This randomness is viewed as a random sample from a given distribution with unknown but fixed parameters.

These assumptions are turned around in the Bayesian approach to probability. In this approach to probability, the parameters are all considered to be random variables with data that is known. The parameters are regarded as coming from a distribution of possible values, and Bayesians look to the observed data to provide information on likely parameter values.

Criticism of the Bayesian framework has focused primarily on two potential drawbacks. First, the elicitation of a prior distribution may be subjective. That is, two different subject matter experts may provide two different prior distributions, which will presumably percolate through to result in two different posterior distributions. The solution to this problem is (1) to select non-informative priors if the choice of priors is controversial and (2) to apply a large amount of data so that the relative importance of the prior is diminished. Failing this, model selection can be performed on the two different posterior distributions using model adequacy and efficacy criteria, resulting in the choice of the better model. Is reporting more than one model a bad thing?

The second criticism has been that Bayesian computation has been intractable in data mining terms for most interesting problems where the approach suffered from scalability issues. The curse of dimensionality hits Bayesian analysis rather hard, given that the normalizing factor requires integrating (or summing) over all possible values of the parameter vector, which may be computationally infeasible when applied directly. The introduction of Markov chains Monte Carlo (MCMC) methods, such as Gibbs sampling and the Metropolis algorithm, has greatly expanded the range of problems and dimensions that Bayesian analysis can handle.

Genetic Algorithms

In the field of genetic algorithms, the candidate solution to any problem is defined using a chromosome, and a gene is synonymous with a single digit in the solution. An allele can be defined as an instance of a digit or a bit, for example, 1 for a binary-encoded solution or the number 4 for a real-value solution.

Genetic algorithms use three operators:

Selection

The selection operator refers to the method used for selecting which chromosomes will be reproducing. The fitness function evaluates each of the chromosomes (candidate solutions), and the fitter the chromosome, the more likely it will be selected to reproduce.

Crossover

You can perform the process of recombination using the crossover operator. This will allow you to create two off springs. When you use this operator, you can select the locus at random and change the locus between the selected chromosomes during the process. If you are using a binary representation of two strings, like 11110000 and 00001111, you can choose the locus at the sixth point in the string and cross the characters over. This will leave you with 11110111 and 00001000.

Mutation

You can use the mutation operator to make changes at random to the digits orbits in the string. This can be done at any locus in the chromosome. Usually, however, it has a very small probability. For example, after crossover, the 11111000 child string could be mutated at locus two to become 10111000. Mutation introduces new information to the genetic pool and protects against converging too quickly to a local optimum.

Most genetic algorithms function by iteratively updating a collection of potential solutions called a population. Each member of the population is evaluated for fitness on each cycle. A new population then replaces the old population using the operators above, with the fittest members being chosen for reproduction or cloning. The fitness function f (x) is a real-valued function operating on the chromosome (potential solution), not the gene, such that the x in f (x) refers to the numeric value taken by the chromosome at the time of fitness evaluation.

Chapter 12

Understanding the Data Science Puzzle

To practice data science in its truest form, you will need to learn mathematics and statistics and also learn some coding skills. If you do not have some knowledge of the aforementioned subjects, you may not be able to work effectively with the data collected.

The demand for data insights in every industry has increased exponentially, which has forced every industry to adopt data engineering and data science. It is because of this that many variations of data science have evolved. It is impossible to identify who is a data scientist. This chapter covers some key components that are part of every data science role.

Collating, querying and, utilizing data

Data engineers capture and collate large volumes of data – structured, semi-structured, and unstructured data. This data cannot be stored in a conventional database since it exceeds its processing capabilities. The data is too big and does not fit the structural requirement of most database architectures. You have to remember that data engineering tasks are different from data science tasks since the latter focuses more on the analysis, visualization, and prediction. When a data scientist collects and collates the data during the process of analysis, they are performing the same functions that a data engineer would perform.

Valuable insights can be generated from single data sources, and these insights can be combined into several sources that deliver contextual information. This information is used to drive informed decisions based on the data. A data scientist works with several datasets that are stored in the database or even different warehouses.

You will need to query the data to extract relevant information from it regardless of how you store that data. Most often, data scientists use the Structured Query Language (SQL) to obtain relevant information from the data. Irrespective of what applications you are using to use data science technologies on data, you will need to use the following file formats only:

CSV (Comma-separated value) file
Every brand of web-based analysis and desktop-based application accepts and uses this file type. Some common scripting languages like Python and R also use this file type.

Scripts
Data scientists often use scripting languages like R and Python, to visualize and analyze data. These languages can only read files that end with the extension .r and .py, respectively.

Application Files

Excel is a tool that can be used to analyze databases that are small or medium-sized. This application saves the files using the following extensions -.xlsx or .xls depending on the size of the data. Other application files save the data using their own file formats.

Web Programming Files

If you are trying to build web-based data visualization files, you will often use data-driven documents or java scripts. The work that you perform will be saved in an .html format.

Using Mathematics and Statistics

Data science relies on the scientist's mathematical and statistical skills since they are needed to understand the data and its significance. These skills are valuable since they can be used to carry out decision modeling, hypotheses testing, and predictive forecasting.

You have to keep in mind that statistics and mathematics are fields that are different from each other but are interdependent. Mathematics uses deductive reasoning and deterministic numerical methods to create a quantitative description of the world while statistics, which is a mathematical science, uses a stochastic approach to arrive at a similar quantitative description of the world.

Applying Mathematical Modeling

Data scientists often use mathematical models to generate approximations, build decision models, and also to make futuristic predictions. Some of the complex mathematical approaches have been covered in later chapters, which are useful to understand.

If you are someone who remembers basic mathematics, you will be able to grasp these approaches with ease. In other words, every approach has been explained using layman terms, making it easy for everyone to understand.

Using Statistical Methods

Statistical methods are used to obtain a better understanding of the data. You will be able to understand the significance of the data and also validate any hypotheses. These methods can be used to predict future events effectively. Most data scientists and engineers are not adept at using advanced statistical skills. If you are keen on moving up the ladder as a data scientist, you must acquire and build on statistical skills like regression, Monte Carlo simulations, time series analysis, and so on. It is not necessary for you to master all these skills, but will need to understand the fundamental concepts to get the most out of your analysis.

Coding

This is one aspect of data science that is unavoidable. You will need to be able to instruct your computer to perform the tasks you need for the data. Languages like R and Python are important to learn when it comes to writing codes and scripts for manipulation, analysis, and visualization of data, while SQL is useful to obtain information using queries.

Coding is a requirement for data science, but it is not as scary as people make it out to be. The code you write can be as complex and fancy as you want it to be since you can take a simple approach. These skills are paramount to succeed in the field of data science, which can be learned through coding.

Applying Data Science to your area

Some statisticians are stubborn when it comes to accepting the significance of the results obtained through data science. They have cried out that there is nothing new about data science. They believe that it is exactly what they have been doing all along. When you look at data science from their perspective, what they are saying may be true. It is also true that data science is distinct and separate from the statistical approaches that it consists of.

Data scientists often use computer languages that are often not used in traditional statistics and also utilize approaches from mathematics. The main distinction between data science and statistics is the need for expertise in the subject – matter.

Since statisticians have limited expertise in fields outside of statistics, they will need to consult a subject – matter expert to understand what their findings mean and to decide on the next step. Data scientists need to have some expertise in the area they are working in. They generate insights and use their area-specific expertise to understand the insights they have obtained. The list below shows how experts use data science to enhance their performance:

- Clinical data scientists work on preparing treatment plans for their patients
- Engineers use machine learning to optimize the efficient use of energy in modern buildings
- Data journalists scrape fresh data from websites to report the latest news
- Marketing data scientists use regression to understand their customers wants and need and also predict their likes and dislikes

Communicating Data Insights

This is another skill set that is paramount to the success of a data scientist. A data scientist will need to have sharp verbal and written communication skills. If you are a data scientist who cannot communicate the insights you have obtained from data, there is no way you will be able to better the functioning of the organization. You will need to explain the insights obtained in layman terms to ensure that your staff members understand what you have obtained and understood. They will also need to be able to produce meaningful and clear data visualizations and written narratives. People often need to be able to see something to understand it. You, as a data scientist, will have to be pragmatic and creative in their methods of communication.

Chapter 13

The Data Science Landscape

L eaders of every organization are trying to understand how they can use data science and big data to their advantage. Most leaders know that analytics can be used to bring a competitive edge to their firm, but there are only a few who know how to extract the right information from data. This chapter discusses the major data science methodologies and solutions and the benefits of data science.

Exploring Data Science Methodologies and Solutions

When you look at different ways to implement data science across a firm or an organization, or even a department, three main approaches can be used. You can outsource the work to an external group of data scientists, use cloud-based solutions or build an in-house data science team that will deliver the power of data analytics to members in the firm who have a modest understanding of data.

Building an in-house team

Three options can be considered when building an in-house data science team.

Train Existing Employees

This is the conservative approach that a firm can take since this method does not cause any costs to the company. If you are keen to equip your firm with the power of data analytics and data science, training the existing staff on data science into becoming subject matter experts is the safest and lower-cost option.

Train Existing Employees and Hire Experts

Another option is to train existing employees and also hire some data scientists to enhance the data insights that are derived from the data collected.

Hire Experts

Some organizations prefer hiring experts or graduates who have a degree in data science. There are not too many people around with these qualifications, and if you do find someone, they will often have high salary requirements.

In addition to understanding mathematics, statistics, and coding, data scientists will need to be experts in the field they are working in. It is hard to find individuals with these skills.

Outsourcing Requirements

Some companies prefer outsourcing their data science requirements to outside experts. There are only two routes that can be taken if companies would prefer this option – outsource the development of data science strategies that would serve the organization or outsource some data scientists if there is any problem that arises within the company.

Outsourcing for Strategy Development

If you would like to build a strategy for your organization, you can hire consultants to help you develop a comprehensive data science strategy. This type of service will cost you, but you will be able to obtain valuable insight from the data in return. Strategists often know about the options that can meet your requirements and also the pros and cons of each option that is being used. You can build an internal team easily if you have an expert who can help you.

Outsourcing for Specific Problems

If you are not prepared to hire experts to build comprehensive data science models, you can choose to outsource smaller portions of the work to different consultants. This could help you reap the benefits of data science without having to reorganize the financials and structure of the entire organization.

Leveraging Cloud-Based Platform Solutions

Some people have seen the explosion of data science and big data coming from a very long way off! These terms are new to a few organizations and professionals, but some are working fast and hard to prepare the world for the explosion. Some organizations and firms have expended effort and expense to develop data science solutions that are accessible to human beings through cloud-based platforms. These platforms are automated data services that do not require any coding. You will still need to understand the statistical, mathematical, and relevance of the data insights.

Identifying the Benefits

Over the course of the book, you will learn about the power of data science and how that power can be used to reach your professional and personal goals. Irrespective of the sector you work in, when you acquire the skills, you will be able to become a marketable professional. The following are the list of benefits of data science that can be delivered across key industry sectors.

Benefits for corporations

The following are the benefits that can be obtained by corporations:

- Production-costs
- Customer lifetime-value increases
- Inventory requirements and sales predictions
- Pricing-model optimization
- Staff-productivity optimization
- Sales maximization
- Marketing ROI increases
- Fraud detection
- Customer-churn reduction
- Optimization
- Logistics improvements

Benefits for Government

Governments benefit from data science in the following ways:

- Finance and budget forecasting
- Fraud detection
- Expenditure tracking and optimization
- Business-process and staff-productivity optimization
- Management decision-support enhancements

Benefits for Academia

Student's benefit from data science in the following ways:

- Business-process optimization
- Drop-out reductions
- Student performance management improvement
- Finance and budget forecasting and recruitment
- Resource-allocation improvements
- ROI increases

Chapter 14

Common Data Science Tools

It has been mentioned earlier that programming is a very integral part of data science. This does not mean that if you do not know to code, you are doomed. There are a number of people who enter the field of data science but do not have great knowledge of the different programming languages that can be used. There are a number of tools that have been developed that do not require any coding at all. These tools avoid the aspect of programming using user-friendly GUI so that a person with minimal knowledge of programming and algorithms will be able to build predictive models. Let us take a look at some of these tools.

Data Robot

Data Robot, or DR, is a machine-learning platform that is highly automated. It was built by Owen Zhang, Jeremy Achin, and Thoman DeGodoy. The founder believed that the role of a data scientist is now obsolete because of the platform. The benefits of DR have been listed below:

Model Optimization

You can use this platform to identify the right way to process any information by using variable type detection, text mining, imputation, encoding, transformation, and scaling. It also chooses parameters depending on the validation set score.

Deployment

One would need to click on a few buttons to deploy their data analyses. They would not need to write any code.

Parallel Processing

The computing power of this platform has been divided across multiple servers. These servers use a variety of algorithms to process large datasets.

For Engineers

Software engineers can integrate different languages into the platform.

Google Cloud Prediction API

You can use this platform to build machine-learning models for any android application. This is a tool that was built specifically for mobiles. Some of the uses of this platform include:

Recommendation Engine

The platform can be used to predict what products or movies a user may want to view based on the user's viewing habits.

Spam Detection

This platform will learn to categorize emails as spam.

Sentiment Analysis

The platform helps data scientists identify if their predicted future has a positive or negative tone.

Purchase Prediction

Using this platform, a data scientist can identify how much a user may spend on any given day based on his purchasing history.

Paxata

Paxata is an organization that focuses on data cleaning and preparation and not just the machine learning or modeling aspect. It is an application similar to Microsoft Excel and is extremely easy to use. It uses visual guidance to help the user bring the data together, find missing data, and fix any errors within the data. It also helps the user share and reuses the data across different projects and teams. Paxata eliminates the need for coding, thereby helping the user overcome any technical barriers.

The following processes are followed in Paxata:

- Data is collated using a wide range of sources.
- The data is then explored using visuals, which allow the user to identify the gaps in the data.
- The data is cleaned using steps like the normalization of similar values, imputation, and detecting duplicates.

- Pivots are created using the data where similar data are grouped and aggregated.
- The data is then shared across teams where different analyses are performed.
- Data is then combined using a proprietary technology – SmartFusion – that combines the data with just one click. This technology detects the best combination and allows multiple datasets to be combined.
- Business Intelligence (BI) tools are used to visualize the combined data. This also allows for iterations to take place between the processing of data and visualization.

RapidMiner

RapidMiner (RM) was started in the year 2006 as a standalone, and an open-source software called Rapid- I. Developers and engineers have continued to develop this software after it received a funding of 35 million USD. The latest version of this tool is not an open-source version, and you will need to purchase the license after a fourteen-day trial period.

RM covers the complete cycle of predictive modeling right from the preparation of data to building a model for that data and finally validating and visualizing that data. RapidMiner is like Simulink and uses a block-diagram interface. Certain blocks are predefined to act as play and plug devices, and you will need to connect these dots in the right manner. You will also be able to run numerous algorithms on RM without using any code. RM also allows for Python and R scripts to be integrated into the system.

The current product offers the following:

RapidMiner Cloud

This is a cloud-based repository that allows for information to be shared between different devices.

RapidMiner Server

This is an environment that has repositories that allow for a team to work on data at the same time and also model the deployment of data visualization.

RapidMiner Radoop

This software implements and incorporates big data analytics methodologies and techniques through Hadoop.

RapidMiner Studio

This is standalone software that can be used to prepare data, visualize data, and also perform statistical modeling on the data.

Chapter 15

Predictive Analytics 101

The field of predictive analytics is one that runs entirely on the data available. There can never be too much data. It is a good idea to have more knowledge about something. This will enable you to make more informed decisions (often more accurate). This is especially true when you need to make some predictions. When you have more information, the accuracy of the predictions you make will be higher. Consider the following example: you are on a game show. The game is very simple and basically requires picking one out of 5 doors. There is a reward only behind one door. The probability of you choosing the right door is 1/5. If you had any information regarding the doors and what lies behind them, you can make an educated guess, which would undoubtedly increase your chances of winning the prize. Predictive analytics is based on this idea of using data at your disposal to make predictions.

Exploring Predictive Analytics

If you were to know what the future holds for you for certain, you would start to lead your life very differently. How will your life change if you were to win the lottery next year? Ideally, you would start to plan for your life ahead, and since you had the one-year of planning, the odds are that you would lead a very peaceful life. By simply knowing something that would happen a year later, you would be able to live a much more efficient life. Predictive analytics allows you to do this to some extent (because you cannot tell for sure what will happen). Think about it this way - If you could forecast every moment in your life, you will learn to make the most of each moment. It could be considered to be somewhat of a superpower. You would be able to lead a successful and efficient life without ever running into any problems! This might sound a little dull to people who enjoy the adrenaline rushes of gambling and other uncalculated risks. People who are focused on being successful and rich would go to any length to have this ability. You will build on this ability when you work on predictive analytics.

Mining Data

In recent times, almost everyone in the world would have come across the term "big data." This means that there is too much data in the world, and it is true. We must learn to make use of the information that one can find out there.

Data is an extremely valuable asset for anyone. Many large companies around the world have special data analytics sectors so that they can acquire as much useful data as possible. The keyword here is useful. We need to be able to extract out of all the welter of data only that data which is relevant to us. This is called data mining. It is the procedure of finding patterns and traits in the data using machine learning algorithms. Then predictive analytics comes into play. You need to analyze the information to make educated predictions about future events. So, to summarize, we need to use data mining along with predictive analytics to extract value from a set of data.

Numerous companies across the globe focus on data mining. The goal is to accumulate all the data, analyze it, and identify different methods that will help the business perform better than its competitors. This information also helps businesses optimize their operations. Companies also use this data to figure out how to expand their customer base and increase their market share in the process. How can they improve their stronghold in the marketplace? How can they use this data to enhance their competitive edge? Companies have been successful in figuring all of this out by using data mining and predictive analytics.

The tool of predictive analytics is not restricted to the sphere of the business alone. For instance, it has been employed by governments as well. Law enforcement agencies use this tool to figure out whether or not a person is a suspect. They track his movements and behavior and use this data to infer whether or not he is a criminal. Anti-terrorist organizations also use predictive analytics. They look at past data and try to make predictions about where the terrorists might attack next. Even sports organizations can use predictive analytics. A football coach may watch the tapes of his opponent to decipher the plays they run. This would put his team in a better position to win the game. Even students use predictive analytics, albeit on a smaller scale. When a big exam is coming up, students often look into the papers from previous years and try to predict what type of questions may be asked. This tool is in use in various spheres of life simply because any information about the future can put us in a much better position to make the most of it.

Highlighting the Model

Almost every phenomenon in the world has a mathematical model. These models are simply representations of the phenomenon. The advantage of models is that they can be used to investigate the phenomenon further and learn more about it. Consider a sales company. They will look to model the behavior of their customers. They accomplish this by emulating how the customers shop and browse through their webpage (if one exists). Some of the questions they use as building blocks to the model are:

- Have they read the reviews provided by users?
- The number of reviews read
- Whether both positive and negative reviews were read
- Were there any products they looked at before making a purchase?
- Did the customers purchase a product apart from the one that they were looking for?
- Did they view any pages before they made the purchase?
- Did they look at the products' descriptions?

The answers to all these questions are obtained from the analysis of past data. The company stores all the transactions and history of customers, and it uses different tools to identify patterns and trends that will provide answers to the above questions. The collection of the data is an important step, as well. Just collecting all the data and storing it will make the analysis extremely complicated. The company needs to set limits on the breadth and depth of data and the quality level. These limits will define the structure of the model and also the outputs expected.

The entire process of predictive analytics should not be confused with simply looking at the data and reporting whatever appears to the naked eye. These are just parts of the process of obtaining the data and extracting useful and important information from it.

Let us now come to the topic of how to approach any predictive analytics problem. It is advisable to follow a systematic procedure. This way, we will get the desired results from the process. The following are the steps involved:

- Take time to understand the problem you are trying to solve completely. This understanding is extremely important.
- Accumulate the relevant data and collate it so that examining it will become easier.
- Now run data mining algorithms, machine learning algorithms, and other tools of statistical analysis on the data.

You should only look at that data, which is useful for the process. The data mining step is of utmost importance. Then you are required to run various algorithms on the data, which are step-by-step procedures that help you to arrive at a solution. The idea is to go through various combinations of data and try to answer several what-if scenarios. Build a mathematical model, run these algorithms, and use the answers to make the most of the future events.

For someone who has not used mathematical models ever, the question of what a model looks like arises. If you are familiar with programming terminology, you can use simple conditional statements. These statements could be used to instruct the machine to perform a specific function if something were to happen. If that doesn't happen, THEN do something else. Here is a simple example: If on a particular day, the market is up, then buy some shares of ABC. If at any point the stock is up by 10 percent, then sell the stock and earn the profits. Else, exit your position or wait until the stock goes up again.

Consider the example of an online shoe store. A model for this store could look something like this:

- If you see a user buy a shoe from one brand, you can recommend other products from the same brand.
- If you see a user purchase a shoe for a specific purpose (for example, casual, party wear, etc.), you can recommend other shoes that fit the purpose.
- If a user has purchased a pair of shoes, recommend those shoes that were purchased by other customers who have a similar taste. Adding Business Value

The competition in the business sector has been on the rise in the last few years. In such times, it is always incumbent upon the company to find new ways to outperform their competitors. Predictive analytics is a tool that can help companies achieve this goal. Companies can use data mining algorithms; machine learning algorithms, and other tools of statistical analysis to help them process large volumes of data. These algorithms will make it easier to extract the patterns and trends in the data set. Businesses that use these tools have a competitive edge in the market.

The usage of predictive analytics in making operational decisions can help increase the return on investment for a company. Companies will spend lesser time working with low impact and low-risk aspects and start focusing on the high impact and high-risk ones. For instance, almost all standard insurance claims can be paid out automatically. The claim will be flagged if the company uses a predictive modeling tool that can identify the outliers or any unusual claims. The company can then call upon the person responsible for the claim and take the necessary action.

As mentioned earlier, a company can use predictive analytics in order to predict future events. This way, the company can prepare for that event and put itself in an advantageous position to make the most of it. For example, a shoe company can increase the number of sports shoes in the store during the Soccer World Cup because the demand will increase. This way, they can cater to the demands of their customers and also have increased sales. The eighth law of data mining proposed by Tom Khabaza speaks about this as well.

This law states that the value of any predictive model can be calculated on the basis of two attributes:

1. The accuracy of the prediction

2. The new information provided by the model

Endless Opportunities

Businesses want to use optimization algorithms to manage their inventories and allocation of resources among employees better. They want to make their planning process more dynamic. These companies are looking to pounce on opportunities and make the most out of them.

The use of predictive analytics can achieve all these goals. As explained in earlier sections, predictive analytics can be applied in various spheres ranging from business to sports organizations. Companies should invest in data mining and predictive analysis because if they do not, at least a few of their competitors will employ these tools and get ahead of them.

One of the greatest minds to have ever lived, Albert Einstein, once said, "Know where to find information and how to use it as that is the secret of success." This is the basic idea behind predictive analytics. The goal is to find information and use it to our benefit. So, according to Einstein's quote, using predictive analytics will make you successful. You will need to use data mining, as well. Once you have the data you need, interpreting it is solely based on how good your knowledge of your field is. This knowledge is extremely important in finding valuable information in the data provided to you. Once you can correctly analyze your data and come up with predictions, you will become successful.

Empowering your organization

The previous sections have discussed and concluded that predictive analytics would help make your company more successful. But how? The following are the three major advantages provided by the use of predictive analytics.

Vision

The first advantage provided by the tool is the vision. Businesses can use these tools to look for patterns or trends that will give them a competitive edge in the market. It can yield results that can give your company and insight into the future. This insight will help in preparing your company so that it can make the best of the future. This can help increase profits and also increase your customer base.

Predictive analytics will look through past data of your customers and can relate it to other data that exists. It will then look to assemble this data in a manner such that it can help solve problems. The following are some examples of how the tool arranges the data:

- Guessing your customers' next actions.
- Knowing your customers' wish lists.
- Categorizing your customers as loyal, seasonal, or wandering.
- Categorizing your customers and speculating about their needs.

Decision

There can be a bias when human beings decide to make decisions based on data. A predictive analytics model makes decisions that are free from bias and emotion. The model looks at past information and uses that data to make calculations and predictions. Hence, the results of a predictive analytics model are completely unbiased.

Banks also use predictive analytics for various reasons. One of the most common applications of the tool is for the banks to predict the creditworthiness of a person in the future. Based on this, banks decide whether or not to extend someone's credit or grant them a new credit card. If this were to be done by an employee of the bank, it would not be surprising to see that his decisions had some shades of bias in them.

Precision

Let us once again compare a person and a model working on predictive analytics. As mentioned earlier, one of the main steps is data mining. Data mining requires going through tons of data and picking out only the relevant data. There will be errors if a human being manually mines data since there is a lot of data for them to look at. On the other hand, a model that uses a data-mining algorithm will be able to achieve this goal faster and with more accuracy. Also, if you wanted it to be done manually, you would need to hire more than one person for the job. This way, you end up wasting resources as well. Hence, using automated tools for predictive analytics will help cut costs, reduce errors, and also save time and resources. The precision that comes with using these automated tools gives rise to other benefits as well. For instance, if you were looking to launch a new product and wanted to know which customers to target. By using predictive analytics and looking at past consumer behavior, you can pick the customers you want to target, and this could lead to higher sales.

Starting a Predictive Analytics Project

Now that you know the advantages of using predictive analytics, let us now talk about how to start your predictive analytics project. Let us keep all the arcane algorithms and math aside for a second. Humans have used predictions in many aspects of their lives for many years now. Weather forecasts are one of the most common examples. Even the common man uses prediction in daily life (remember the example of the student preparing for an examination).

If we want any accuracy out of these predictions, we will have to consider the past as well. Making predictions off the top of our heads without examining any data will rarely lead to any accuracy. You need to follow a certain procedure:

- Look through information and filter out the facts that are related to the problem
- Take your time to separate the current facts from the past facts
- After analyzing the data and looking for trends, try making predictions about what might happen

- Make multiple predictions and rank them in order of likeliness of occurrence.

This is where you can use predictive analytics. It can help you with each of the steps mentioned above. This way, you will have all the information you need about the problem at hand, which makes it easier for you to predict the outcome with higher accuracy.

When companies conduct predictive analysis, they use three key ingredients to arrive at their solutions:

- Business knowledge
- Data-science team and technology
- Data

Companies have the freedom to give more importance to one of the above factors when compared to others. A minimum focus on all three factors is essential to run successful predictive analytics.

Business Knowledge

The coach of a football team cannot become a coach without any knowledge of the sport. A Wall Street broker cannot become successful without any knowledge of the stock market. Similarly, for someone to run a predictive analytics project to fulfill some business needs, he needs to have some level of business knowledge. You cannot expect to obtain the desired results if you do not have the required knowledge. The leadership and management team of a company need to be well versed in the concepts of business.

It is important to ensure that the people using the tool to make decisions are willing to act. In a company, when someone presents an innovative idea, there needs to be a member of the management who believes in it and who will push for it. Similarly, the predictions made by the predictive analytics tool need to be adopted by the management, and this will only happen if they are ready to act upon those predictions.

The management and leadership team should also be held responsible for setting goals (quantifiable goals). Unless you can measure the outcome of the predictive analytics tool, you will not know if it is working as desired. Also, metrics will help keep employees determined to reach the goal. It gives them feedback as to whether or not they are doing what is expected of them.

Consult the stakeholders in the business. Generally, these are the people with the greatest knowledge in the field, and their advice can improve the functions of the tool. They will be aware of what patterns to look for. They will also provide information on which variables you should focus on when looking for trends. In case other variables need to be added to the model, the stakeholders will know which ones to pick. Finally, they can also look at the results of the tool and analyze them. Since they have a lot of knowledge in the field, they will be able to interpret the data accurately and will also be able to provide valuable predictions.

Data Science and Technology

The tools that you will use for predictive analytics should include at least 3 of the following four capabilities (all four would be advisable):

- Statistical analysis tools
- Machine learning algorithms
- Data mining
- Software used to build the model

As mentioned in the previous section, you want the decision-makers to be well versed in business concepts. They need not necessarily understand the technology that has been used for making the model. All they need to know is what the model is supposed to represent and have a good understanding of that. The data scientists (people who generate the model and conduct data mining) and the management should communicate regularly.

It is advisable to train the data scientists in the basic concepts of business. This will help them in generating a much more efficient model. Increased efficiency in the model can translate to better and more accurate results from the predictive analysis. Also, this basic knowledge will allow the data scientists to expedite the process. The model can be used to obtain results when it is developed fully. By collaborating with the management teams, data scientists will know if their model is working correctly. It is recommended that the data scientists know a little bit about business, and the management teams know a little bit about data science.

An important stage in the process is the selection of the software for running the analysis. The following factors come into play at this stage:

- The complexity of data
- The source of the data
- The complexity of the business problem
- The variability of the data
- The cost of the product
- The people within the organization who will use the product

Data

The advantages that experience comes with cannot be overstated. When looking at two candidates for a job, you would certainly want to pick the one who has more experience in the field (assuming all other qualifications are equal). The same concept can be applied to an organization. If we look at an organization as a person, the amount of experience translates to the amount of data at the organization's disposal. With more data, you can perform a more thorough analysis and hence, more accurate results. Therefore with greater data, you can make more insightful decisions. It should now be evident that data is very important in predictive analysis. Data helps in giving more effective results.

In its raw form, data poses several challenges. You must learn to pick the right data for your analysis. Data can be distributed across multiple sources, making it harder to accumulate. Sometimes data gets mixed with other third-party data, and this makes the segregation process complex. So, data scientists need to spend substantial amounts of time cleaning up the data and picking only that, which is useful. You must look for extremities, duplicates, outliers, abnormalities, and missing data.

Big data also has some inherent qualities that can be very challenging. Some of these are volume, number of types, and variability. There is too much data that comes in too fast from different sources. All these qualities come together to make the job of data mining difficult. You need to remove important information from this cluster.

There are many algorithms that you can use to mine data. Which of these algorithms should you choose? The team responsible for data science needs to analyze the data and its type. Based on this, they need to select an algorithm that will best suit their needs. You should also ensure that you pay attention to the data set and choose the right algorithm for that data set.

Conclusion

Data analytics and data science have taken the world by storm, and people have been trying to use these methods to improve their lifestyles. There are numerous businesses, big and small, that are using these techniques to improve their businesses. If you wanted to learn more about data analytics and the different concepts of data analytics, you could use this book as a guide.

Thank you for purchasing the book. I wish you luck on your journey.

Sources

https://www.techopedia.com/definition/26418/data-analytics

https://www.simplilearn.com/data-science-vs-big-data-vs-data-analytics-article

https://data36.com/data-analytics-basics-intro/

https://www.snp.com/blog/8-ways-data-analytics-can-improve-your-business

https://www-935.ibm.com/services/in/gbs/business-analytics/

https://www.pwc.com/gx/en/issues/data-and-analytics/improve-business-performance.html

https://firstround.com/review/how-to-consistently-hire-remarkable-data-scientists/

https://bigdata-madesimple.com/how-you-can-improve-customer-experience-with-fast-data-analytics/

https://www.business.com/articles/build-brand-loyalty-with-big-data/

https://www.sas.com/en_si/insights/articles/marketing/how-to-build-customer-loyalty-in-four-steps.html

https://becominghuman.ai/predicting-buying-behavior-using-machine-learning-a-case-study-on-sales-prospecting-part-i-3bf455486e5d

https://www.optimove.com/learning-center/customer-behavior-modeling

https://towardsdatascience.com/decision-trees-in-machine-learning-641b9c4e8052

https://www.upgrad.com/blog/association-rule-mining-an-overview-and-its-applications/

https://www.scaleunlimited.com/about/web-mining/

https://www.techopedia.com/definition/3205/social-network-analysis-sna

http://www.orgnet.com/sna.html

https://searchbusinessanalytics.techtarget.com/definition/data-visualization

https://www.dataquest.io/blog/data-science-glossary/

http://neuralnetworksanddeeplearning.com/

https://skymind.ai/wiki/neural-network

https://www.digitalocean.com/community/tutorials/an-introduction-to-machine-learning

https://towardsdatascience.com/introduction-to-machine-learning-db7c668822c4

https://www.forbes.com/sites/bernardmarr/2016/12/06/what-is-the-difference-between-artificial-intelligence-and-machine-learning/#6858e6a02742

https://www.marutitech.com/artificial-intelligence-and-machine-learning/

https://www.marutitech.com/artificial-intelligence-and-machine-learning/

https://www.tutorialspoint.com/artificial_intelligence/artificial_intelligence_overview.htm

https://www.sciencedirect.com/journal/artificial-intelligence

https://www.sas.com/en_in/insights/analytics/what-is-artificial-intelligence.html

https://www.sas.com/en_us/insights/big-data/what-is-big-data.html

https://searchdatamanagement.techtarget.com/definition/big-data

https://www.oracle.com/big-data/guide/what-is-big-data.html

https://www.ibm.com/analytics/hadoop/big-data-analytics

https://www.webopedia.com/TERM/B/big_data.html

https://searchbusinessanalytics.techtarget.com/definition/predictive-analytics

https://www.webopedia.com/TERM/P/predictive_analytics.html

https://www.predictiveanalyticstoday.com/what-is-predictive-analytics/

https://www.sas.com/en_us/insights/analytics/predictive-analytics.html

https://www.healthcatalyst.com/predictive-analytics

https://www.nytimes.com/2004/11/14/business/yourmoney/what-walmart-knows-about-customers-habits.html

www.ingramcontent.com/pod-product-compliance
Lightning Source LLC
LaVergne TN
LVHW051243050326
832903LV00028B/2539